The Enlightened Empath

ALLYSON BLYTHE

LCSW & Certified Life Coach

ISBN 978-1-960378-00-2 (paperback)
ISBN 978-1-960378-01-9 (eBook)
ISBN 978-1-960378-04-0 (hardcover)

1st edition

Book design by Anna Hall

THE ENLIGHTENED EMPATH

CONTENTS

Introduction

My legs couldn't seem to move fast enough as the abrupt surge of anxiety and uneasiness took hold of me. The privacy and sanctuary of the restroom stall greeted me like an old, unwanted friend. My fingers gripped the cold, hard metal lock of the stall door as it slid securely into place.

You've got to be kidding me. As I took a seat on the infamous throne, my internal voice was as unnerving as the overwhelming emotion flooding through my body. *You're a grown woman and you're locking yourself in the bathroom stall again. You've sure come a long way.*

Outside my little fortress, a lovely spring afternoon event had begun, one meant to celebrate and honor women doing amazing things in the community—highly accomplished, dressed-to-the-nines women who were showing up to chat, connect, hug, and share. Then, there was me, locked in the bathroom stall, trying to pull it together because sometimes people are just far too "people-y" for my comfort.

Large groups, chatter, superficial smiles, and insincere conversation were all too much for me to handle. Often, the best path to solace was to perch myself in a public restroom, waiting for the overwhelm and overstimulation to pass until I could somehow muster the strength to return to my seat at that dreaded lunch table. I'd been doing the same kind of thing since I was a teen.

I couldn't help it, and for years, I couldn't explain it. Those were agonizing, condemning years that left me embarrassed, confused, and avoiding any type of setting that would evoke that sense of uncertainty and overwhelm. Unfamiliar situations plagued me from the time I was little. The sensations would come as a riddled sense of flooding, exhaustion, and depletion that seemed to emerge from nowhere whenever I experienced too much—too much noise, energy, emotion, light, stimulation, conversation, too much of anything. I had no understanding, no filter, and no way to process what I was experiencing, nor could I make sense of anything that was happening.

Everyone else seemed to enjoy these experiences. Everyone would chat, exchange numbers, and pose with those dreaded forced smiles. Yet, time and time again, I could be found hiding in the bathroom, inundated with feelings of doubt, hesitation, and overwhelm. Social situations often created drastic shifts of mood and energy inside of me, leaving me feeling crazy and unpredictable. Crowds felt chaotic and engulfing because I felt things no one else seemed to feel, sensed things no one else seemed to sense, and *knew* things no one else seemed to know. Why? What was all of this?

Why, all during childhood and still decades later, had I not figured out a better public coping mechanism than taking refuge in the safety and comfort of those four bathroom stall walls?

Get it together! my inner critic jabbed.

And so I did. I collected myself enough to find my footing, muster a smile, and maneuver my way back to the table to finish out the uncomfortable afternoon. It was always like this for me. No matter how I tried, I couldn't seem to arrive at a solution to the problem.

A WORD THAT CHANGED EVERYTHING

I'm a mental health professional, and over the years, I've run the gamut of trying to diagnose the unlimited possibilities and categories of what could be wrong with me. I remember sitting with the DSM (*Diagnostic and Statistical Manual of Mental Health Disorders*), trying to make sense of it all as I flipped through the hundreds of pages. Was this bipolar disorder? Depression? Social anxiety? Insecurity and self-doubt? Or was I just a total freak of nature? I had seriously considered all those options more than once, and every time I came up empty, that inner critic never failed to chime in with its defeating chatter and ridicule. *What's wrong with me?* was a question that echoed through my mind daily.

But then I stumbled upon a word that changed everything. I don't know when or how it happened, but I was introduced to a word, a concept, that forever altered the lens through which I see myself. It was a term that suddenly brought my entire existence into sharp focus. I had certainly heard the word before but never understood the depth or intensity of what it meant to be described with it. The word: *Empath*—here defined as more than the feeling of empathy, but as a human being who experiences the world in an intense, profound way, one who can absorb the emotion and energy of others, of things, and of environments, and be impacted by them in the mind, body, and spirit.

3

The gift of understanding suddenly allowed me to see my life differently, and decades of suffering, turmoil, and self-loathing came to a screeching halt. Just as a person struggling to see becomes fitted with proper glasses or a person challenged to hear is offered hearing aids to effectively take in sound, I had a new perspective with which to fully comprehend what was really "wrong with me."

As a matter of fact, there was nothing wrong. I just hadn't understood it properly. No one in my life had, until now. I was not a freak of nature. It was not a mental health issue, nor was I an insecure, incapable woman.

I was (and am) an Empath.

All those years of emotional exhaustion and depletion, those layers of social uncertainty, the thousands of unexplained tears shed (sometimes for people I didn't even know), the high levels of sensitivity, and the rapidly shifting emotions were all suddenly explained through that one simple word: *Empath*. I still feel the liberation.

If you can identify with any of the above, I ask you this:

- Are you a deep feeler, often sensing and perceiving things that others don't?
- Have you ever been called too sensitive or been encouraged to toughen up?
- Do people describe you as "too much"?
- Have you been plagued by the distress and anguish of our world?
- Are you struggling to find support and community in a world that feels heavy?
- Have you had a lifetime of being deeply affected by things that happen around you?

My friend, if your answer to any of these questions is yes, then you too may be an Empath, and your journey is about to begin!

This book is for you, the deep feelers of the world, the people who sense things, know stuff, and are tenderhearted. I know you're out there because I see you, I meet with you in my office, and I am one of you too. I know the reality of living as a disempowered Empath—the depletion, confusion, exhaustion, and overwhelm. I understand the toll the world can take on your mind, body, spirit, and soul. Even as a therapist and life coach—one who has visited with thousands of clients over the years, built a successful practice, read most of the self-help books, written a self-help book, taken the courses, created and taught the courses, even earned the degrees hanging on the wall—I had no understanding of who I was, how I was wired, or what seemed to be wrong with me.

Like you, I *feel* life. I *feel* the people who cross my path. My emotions are big, my reactions are strong, and my perspective is deep. I know things that I don't know how I know. I sense things and can put pieces and perceptions together to enhance that *knowing*. These skills make me really good at what I do and really effective at helping the people I work with. Yet, when not managed or regulated properly, those same skills can plague my spirit and suck the life out of me.

A disempowered Empath is a depleted, destructive Empath. I know because I was one, and it created chaos in my mood, thoughts, behaviors, and relationships. It took years of learning and exploring, along with loads of self-work, trial-and-error practices, and lots of live-and-learn experiences to understand what my *issue* was. It took even longer to determine the verbiage, tools, and coping mechanisms to enhance my capabilities and step into the empowered realm of being an Empath.

This book is the culmination of that journey, and I look forward to sharing it with you.

WITH GREAT POWER COMES GREAT RESPONSIBILITY

Let's start by acknowledging some basic truths. Our world is hurting. We're amid deep rivers of change, facing seasons of discord, fear, and uncertainty. People are scared and suffering. Everywhere you look, you can see the devastation that exists in our world. Equally tragic are the ways some humans treat one another. For some people and cultures, "different" often equates to "wrong." People can objectify and vilify anyone who looks or thinks differently. The divide among us is wreaking havoc in our souls. We're so plagued by the pollution in our world, minds, and hearts that sometimes it's hard to come up for air.

Though the world is hurting, and we are facing tragic conditions, all is not lost. The time is now, and the time is perfect for you to step up and step into your empowered role. The world needs you, your voice, your energy, your vision, and your efforts. You are here to do this work and reinspire love, cooperation, and connection. You are here to evolve. You are not broken, nor are you alone. Together, we can make a difference.

In a world where it sometimes seems impossible to find wisdom, resources, and guidance on how to live as an Empath, the pages to come will provide insights designed to inspire hope, action, and a collective movement to support you in turning the energetic tide. It is through this process that you will be educated, equipped, and empowered to utilize your gift, manage your experiences, and relate to others in healthy ways as you build a community of people who are stronger together. You are being called to form a new path, a new way of thinking and connecting so the world can feel tolerable, even enjoyable to you. Collectively, we will do wonders!

This work will allow you to learn, process, share, and grow to help the world become a better place, starting with you. As an Enlightened Empath, you assume a position of strength, capability, and confidence in relationships, experiences, and decision-making as you embrace the power and beauty of who you are and the capability you have.

Hear this clearly. You are not broken, and there's nothing wrong with you. Despite what you've been told, or messages you have received during your life, you were created to be exactly the way you are. Though you may not know it yet, you've been gifted with certain gifts, powers, and abilities. These are your birthrights, and you are here to evolve in your utilization of, and effectiveness with, them. You've come into this world with unique wiring and skills that are critical to understand, accept, and embrace. Every step along the way has led you right here. Every circumstance, struggle, loss, relationship, conversation, and decision has offered information and guidance. You are exactly who, what, and where you need to be.

Perhaps you are arriving here deeply inspired and ready for this calling. Perhaps you are dragging yourself here in a desperate attempt to gain understanding, hope, or definitive action. Either way, this is your call to action as you deepen your understanding of who you are and the gifts you have to offer yourself and the world.

During our time together, we will be exploring the many different facets of being an Empath and determine how each component applies to you. This is intended to awaken you to your abilities, greatness, and personal truth. This work will enable you, if you so choose, to step into your personal power as you learn specific tools, build healthy community and connection, and align with a Source greater than yourself to support you as you develop and employ the gifts you've been granted.

Welcome to the journey!

❧ ARE YOU AN EMPATH?

You've likely spent most of your life being measured, assessed, and told what you are or are not. Perhaps you've looked to outside sources to define and explain you. This assessment is different. It empowers you to understand, claim, and embrace your gifts and struggles through your own evaluation and determination.

This exercise will help you clarify your specific skills and insights. You may find that most, some, or only a few of these apply to you. We're just here to take a look. Let's see if we can shine some light on this exceptional gift to see what applies to you and to what degree.

Write a number from 0-10 in each question's box using the scale below. Then, add up your answer from each question and put it in the TOTAL box at the end.

0 1 2 3 4 5 6 7 8 9 10

NOT AT ALL   SOMEWHAT   ABSOLUTELY

	I experience very deep feelings.
	I feel like a sponge, absorbing energy and experiences around me.
	People tell me I'm too sensitive.
	I have a strong sense of responsibility.
	Strangers relate to me, tell me their problems, or ask my opinion.
	I've always felt different from other people.
	I never really feel like I fit in anywhere.
	I notice things most people don't.

Sometimes I worry that I'm too much for other people.	
I can sense people's feelings and needs, often without them saying anything.	
I can feel other people's pain—emotional or physical.	
I learn differently than others and have to take in information in my own way.	
I struggle to comprehend or retain things I hear or read.	
I often know what someone needs, sometimes before they do.	
I can read someone's energy more than their words.	
I'm thoughtful and conscious of people's needs and feel troubled when others aren't the same way.	
I have a sense of knowing about situations and people.	
I can read energy in a room and the people in it.	
It can be hard to be in my body because of the intense things I feel.	
Sometimes I numb or distract myself to lessen the intensity of my feelings.	
I'm aware of even subtle changes in energy, environment, or someone's mood.	
My mood can shift suddenly and without apparent reason.	
I seem to know things before they happen.	
I have a hard time witnessing violence, aggression, or negativity.	
I startle easily.	
Unfairness and injustice are big triggers for me.	
The energy of crowds impacts me.	

	I don't like small talk.
	A lot of activity is overwhelming to me.
	Tone of voice, body language, and gestures impact the way I relate and communicate.
	Noise, lighting, and activity influence my mood and focus.
	I need quiet, downtime, and solitude to recoup.
	I feel drained and depleted by a lot of activity and busyness.
	Structure and order help me think straight.
	I'm overwhelmed by clutter and other distractions.
	Sometimes committed plans feel overwhelming and suffocating.
	I don't do well with rushing, busyness, and lateness.
	Sudden changes or distractions can really throw me off course.
	It seems to take me longer to recuperate from stress and difficult people.
	Personal space is important to me.
	Sometimes I need to check out when there's a lot going on.
	Conflict and arguments are unsettling to me.
	Competition and performance are draining to me.
	Sarcasm and teasing trouble me.
	I'm sensitive to chemicals, caffeine, and medications.
	I have a strong reaction to physical pain.
	My thoughts and ideas are complex, and I can get lost in them.

I'm deeply moved by music, art, creativity, dance, etc.

News, media, advertisements, television, and reading material affect me.

World events impact me even though I've never met those involved.

Weather affects my mood greatly.

I can feel the power of nature. Trees and plants seem to speak to me.

I see colors or auras around people, places, or things.

I can see light that others can't.

I relate to animals deeply.

I hear things other people don't hear.

I see things other people don't see.

I smell things other people don't smell.

I sense things other people don't sense.

I know things other people don't know.

Total number that apply to me:

The highest possible score for this assessment is 600. Though there is no specific number that qualifies you as an Empath, the higher your score, the more empathically wired you are. This tool allows you to self-define your empathic abilities, an understanding that will be useful as we move through the growing process presented in the chapters to come.

After completing this exercise, I describe myself as an Empath:

0   1   2   3   4   5   6   7   8   9   10

❧ THE EMPATH SCALE

0 – 99: BEGINNER

You are starting to learn and explore emotions and energy on a basic level. You have some awareness of what different emotions are.

100 – 199: SENTIMENT

You have a general view and understanding of feelings and your opinions about things. You can typically express your feelings and views on simple matters and with people you're comfortable with.

200 – 299: APPRISED

You are informed and knowledgeable of emotional language and can have conversations about your feelings and experiences. You have compassion and understanding for the feelings of others.

300 – 399: REALIZED

You can grasp emotions and energy in yourself and others and clearly understand the meaning and impact of them. You appreciate emotional language, needs, and dynamics.

400 – 499: ASCENDING

You are conscious of emotions and energy in yourself and others and are open to learning more. You appreciate the complex nature of emotions and are willing to navigate relationships, conversations, and conflict.

500 – 600: ENLIGHTENED

You are highly in tune with your emotions, energy, and intuition. You practice the many nuances associated with feelings and are capable of deep insight, understanding, and compassion for yourself and others. You can regulate, detach, and embody emotion without absorbing or becoming plagued by it.

CHAPTER 1

The Educated Empath

Empathic people—dreamers and idealists—have this sort of accidental power. Most spend their early years ridden with self-doubt, insecurity, and people-pleasing habits. But their journey is inevitably derailed when this comfortable life gets uprooted by an unexpected darkness. Suddenly, their trusted methods no longer seem to bring them happiness. At first, this depression convinces them that they might never feel joyful again. But ultimately, it sets them on a quest for something more—for love, justice, and wisdom.

Once this adventure begins, there is no stopping a dreamer.

—UNKNOWN

Have you ever witnessed someone get a paper cut and you cringe at the sensation of that painful wound as though it had happened to you? Have you ever heard about a tragedy and felt struck by the grief and anguish of what the family must be enduring? That feeling is called *empathy.* Though our world seems to be showing less and less of it these days, most people experience some level of this emotion with basic care and consideration for others during times of crisis, pain, or hardship.

Since you're holding this book, chances are good that you can relate to the sentiment of empathy. It's possible that the emotion runs deeper for you than it does for most people—much deeper. What some might describe as "small things" feel big to you. You sense things that no one else seems to be aware of. Sometimes you can't tell the difference between which emotions are genuinely yours versus which emotions belong to others. Thoughts and feelings tend to linger longer and deeper for you and can contaminate your mood. Your energy levels shift for no apparent reason—one minute you're fine, and the next, you're not.

It's possible that these occurrences impact your social life as well. Maybe being around people can be a lot for you at times. You may feel anxious and overstimulated without knowing why, and you sometimes feel the need to check out, if only you knew how to do that. There may be situations where you feel irritated or exhausted, even when you genuinely like the people involved. Maybe you've been told for years that you need to toughen up and stop being so sensitive. You may have questioned hundreds if not thousands of times, *What is wrong with me?* Others may echo that question, equally confused about what you're experiencing and why life can feel like a roller coaster with you.

If any of this sounds familiar, you may be an Empath. You are emotionally and energetically wired in a very rare and dynamic way that influences how you function and relate in the world.

Experiencing life as an Empath can be a double-edged sword. Empaths describe being able to feel, sense, and experience the thoughts, emotions, and struggles of others as though they were their own. Most are big feelers, deep thinkers, and profound perceivers. Though it is an incredible gift to be an Empath, it also can be a lot to bear. It can be painful to experience the world in this way, and yet, this power can be miraculous when used properly.

Empaths are sensitive to emotion and energy. This can make for an amazing avenue through which to relate to others. But that deeper sense

14

for emotion and energy can also make life complicated, overwhelming, and confusing. It is not uncommon for Empaths to feel confused by who they are and the ways they experience and relate to people, places, and events. Their emotions and needs are distinct, a fact which can cause them to feel as if they are operating with a profoundly different operating system compared to others. This operating system is beautifully complicated, with nuances and intricacies that can be easily jumbled and tangled. It deserves special attention and respect and is important to honor, use effectively, and protect diligently.

ADAPTING TO THE EMPATH SUPERPOWER

Imagine your level of empathy as you might a superpower. Armed with a supernatural ability, you can make a profound difference and accomplish mighty feats in the world. On the other hand, used in a different way, this same power can wreak havoc and do more harm than good. When empathy is not managed and regulated, it can be quite destructive to you and others. As an Enlightened Empath, you can use those powers differently to live life from a very intentional place, to align with your strengths and abilities, to enjoy fulfilling relationships, and to effect tremendous good for yourself and others.

Empaths can be like sponges—absorbing the emotions, energy, and experiences of everything around. Social settings, work environments, stressful circumstances, uncertainty, and even basic nuances in day-to-day living can flood the heart and mind of an Empath. Because of this, you've likely learned a wide range of coping mechanisms and adaptations, some healthier than others. It's not uncommon for Empaths to develop an array of strategies and survival skills just to get through the day.

Instinctively, your focus is often on accommodating and appeasing others, far more than taking care of yourself. Your radar is likely tuned outward on people, places, and things, trying to get a "read" or "feel," far more than knowing how to tune that radar inward to assess how something feels to you. This can put you at further risk of dysfunctional ways of coping and relating.

It is critical to evaluate the techniques you've been using and how these have helped or hindered you, especially if you haven't understood what it is you're experiencing. This way, you can assess how well they're serving you, and if necessary, determine how you can connect differently. Being properly equipped with knowledge, awareness, and boundaries will help soften the edges of that double-edged sword of empathy and allow you to function from a strengthened place, rather than feeling riddled by the whims and ways of the world.

Early life experiences, labels, messages, and relationships are highly influential and have shaped you in both positive and negative ways. A community of people—including parents, teachers, peers, or religious leaders who don't understand the experience of an Empath—can misrepresent or misidentify specific beliefs and perspectives about you, often in ways that are not supportive or accurate. Perhaps you've absorbed a lot of misinformation, faulty beliefs, and misinterpreted experiences that have molded the way you see yourself.

Imagine a child who doesn't learn in traditional ways. They have different learning capabilities, and because of the limitations of their parents and/or school system to adapt to and foster these capabilities, the child is labeled "learning disabled"—or far worse, stupid, or lazy. The child is misrepresented not because there's something wrong with the child, but because of the lack of understanding within the system and among the adults.

The same is true for the Empath. Unique in their experiences and perceptions, Empaths tend to stand out, have a harder time fitting in, and often don't feel normal. It is common for them to be labeled as dramatic, intense, needy, too much, and sadly, even crazy, or mentally ill. They can be riddled with confusion and misperception about who they are and what their capabilities may be.

One of the more frequent questions I hear from the Empaths I work with is, "What's wrong with me?" or "Why can't I be like other people?" This perspective often gets solidified within the psyche and belief system of the Empath and is echoed from family, educational, religious, and cultural perspectives.

Other people's opinions matter, whether we care to admit it or not, especially if they are in authority, are a caretaker, or are significant to you in some fashion. It's likely that you've absorbed pieces of information and drawn various conclusions along the way, adopting them into your belief structure as *truth*. You've probably done so without fully understanding or consciously choosing what is accurate for you, and what you want to believe and subscribe to.

With tender hearts and huge levels of compassion for others, some Empaths believe their sole purpose is to care for and attend to others. Heightened senses and perception may make it easy for you to connect with and relate to others' experiences. Intuitive nudges and a sense of empathic *knowing* may be hard to ignore or overlook when you're around people. Without awareness, boundaries, and proper tools, you may confuse someone else's energy and emotion with your own.

One grand element of being an adult is that you get to choose, define, and redecide many different factors in life at any point. The work we will embark upon in the pages to come will empower you to mindfully observe and assess these beliefs, perceptions, and worldviews while considering their impact on your thoughts, behavior, spirit, and energy. This work will awaken and develop your senses and insights as you tap into your intuitive gifts and enhance the ways you experience the world in your unique way.

This is your reality check and wake-up call, your opportunity to become consciously aware of the strengths you have, the powerful ways you were created, and your soul purpose in this world. This is your chance to boldly embrace your gifts and learn to develop, use, and fully own them to enable you to function differently and even thrive from your limitless potential.

EXPLORING THE RANGE

It's important to note that not all Empaths are wired the same way, experience the world in the same capacity, or relate in the same fashion or at the same intensity. Empathy comes with a wide variety of abilities, gifts, struggles, and perceptions, making your experience unique and distinctively your own. Because no two people are alike, it is important for you to understand your own experience of being an Empath and the different ways it influences and impacts you.

Though most humans feel some sort of compassion or concern for others, there is a difference between the feeling of empathy versus being an Empath. Seeing someone in pain or in a difficult situation will evoke tenderness from most people, who will naturally demonstrate some consideration for what another human is experiencing. However, Empaths absorb the energy and emotion of people, places, and things, and in response, can be impacted in both positive and negative ways. For an Empath, what they are witnessing is more than a relatable feeling or perspective; it is as though they are actually feeling and experiencing these things as their own. It can be incredibly intense.

To paint a clearer picture, let's look at the gamut this covers. Below is a broad scale presented in a simplistic way to provide a general perspective of how empathy may be experienced by different folks and to understand the differences between people.

Sociopath —— Insensitive —— Compassionate —— HSP —— Empath

On the far left you find the sociopath, defined as a person without a conscience and incapable of feeling compassion or empathy for others. They are unable to experience tenderness or insight for others' perspectives or problems. You might define someone who is labeled as a psychopath, antisocial, or narcissistic somewhere closer to this side of the spectrum. This far extreme on the scale represents a fairly small portion of our world population.

Continuing along, you will recognize the kind of person who may be insensitive, obtuse, or unaware. We all have moments or situations where we're inconsiderate, self-absorbed, or oblivious to things around us, but the difference is that this doesn't define your personality or character. In times like this, you're not lacking care and concern as the sociopathic person does; you're just unaware and out of touch with things around you.

Follow further down the range and you find compassion right in the middle, where most people land on the continuum. They feel compassion for one another and can empathize with pain, trauma, or stress, and for this reason, consider themselves kind and caring, with a basic level of concern for others. Though they feel some concern for the person or situation, the emotion tends to remain in a manageable proportion and eventually fade.

Moving along this line, we identify what is known as an HSP, or Highly Sensitive Person. HSPs are deep feelers and thinkers who tend to be sensitive to various stimulation and have a limited threshold for social interaction and stress. Though similar to Empaths, HSPs don't absorb or feel the full depths that Empaths do. *Psychology Today* identifies about 15 to 20 percent of the population to be wired as HSP.[1]

Now at the extreme right of the spectrum, we arrive at the Empath. These human beings will sense the emotion, energy, and experience of other people, places, and things. They don't just feel compassion. It is as though the experience is happening to them. Empaths are conscious of even the most minor details, can perceive matters in multiple capacities, and can absorb emotions and energy as they are occurring. Without learning how to properly manage or regulate this ability, Empaths can find themselves riddled with stress and strain that isn't even theirs. A study published by Oxford University Press estimated that only one to two percent of the world population can be categorized as Empath.[2] In my opinion, the number is higher than that. Too many people simply don't know what it is, or worse, have been lost to labels such as "mentally ill," "addicted," "eccentric," and so on. Hence, the critical nature of this work.

---

1   https://www.psychologytoday.com/us/basics/highly-sensitive-person

2   Banissy, Michael J. 2013. Synaesthesia, mirror neurons and mirror-touch. In: E Hubbard and J Simner, eds. The Oxford Handbook of Synaesthesia. Oxford: Oxford University Press, pp. 584-605.

THE SCIENCE BEHIND THE GIFT

Though some people have a spiritual, metaphysical, or even "woo-woo" association with empathic wiring that dismisses or minimizes this important skill, science is beginning to change that perspective. Researchers are in the early stages of understanding the brain development and chemistry linked with empathy, and there is a great deal of learning left to do before we fully understand the science of empathic wiring, but initial research is fascinating.

Recent work regarding mirror neurons is impactful in helping us understand the differences observed in an Empath's brain. In the 1990s, a neuroscientist named Giacomo Rizzolatti was conducting a study of macaque monkeys in which particular brain cells were discovered. The team of Italian researchers found that the brain responded in identical fashion when the subject was observing an action being taken as well as when the subject was completing the action. The term *mirror neurons* was coined for these brain cells to reflect the idea that the neurons fired both when the monkeys grabbed an object or witnessed another monkey grab it.

Later research revealed these same cells exist within the human brain. Scientists believe these neurons are responsible for compassion and the ability to share someone else's emotion or experience.

Researchers are beginning to recognize that Empaths have hyperalert mirror neurons, therefore attuning them into deeper, more complex levels of compassion. This explains why the emotion and sensory experiences of an Empath can be so overwhelming. Because they are constantly taking in information and experiencing life with such vigilance, internal systems can be flooded.

Symptoms both emotional and somatic (herein defined as "symptoms affecting the body") are commonplace for Empaths because that flooding and absorption of emotion and energy is simply too much for their mind and body to effectively manage. Empaths don't have the same filters or guards that other people have to protect them from their emotional and sensory experiences. It's typical that they haven't learned to use effective methods and measures to regulate themselves and are therefore susceptible to exhaustion and depletion. This leads to a sense of overwhelm that is difficult to identify or even recognize what's causing it.

When Empaths question, "Why am I so different from other people?" the answer may lie in understanding these mirror neurons. Science is still evolving to better appreciate the meaning and impact of these, but it is powerful information to validate the experience you may be having.

WHAT IS REGULATION?

Brittany recently received a promotion that came with an offer of more money for doing work she really loved to do. Her team was great, and she was excited to be among community again after a long stint of working from home. Like many of the Empaths who come into my office, she expressed confusion about her moods and energy levels since taking on her new role. She found herself exhausted yet unable to sleep, irritable and apathetic, even though she loved her work. Increasingly she was avoiding social interactions, and even daily chores seemed overwhelming. She couldn't seem to pull herself off the couch. Every day was a struggle to get herself together, to the point where she was worried about the toll on her kids and her career.

As we sat together, she tried to oversimplify her problem by claiming that she just needed more rest. But rest never seemed to fix the problem. Her family and friends suggested she was depressed. Her doctor wanted to try her on a low dose of medication. The many different perspectives and opinions were weighing heavily and left her asking that proverbial Empath question: "What's wrong with me?"

Her sessions with me revealed that her empathic wiring was being impacted by the new demands on her time and energy, further affected by a lack of boundaries and self-care. Her work promotion required longer hours, a significant commute in busy city traffic, an unpredictable schedule influencing her ability to plan and maintain a consistent routine, and more customer-facing experiences, often with people who were upset or disgruntled. Excited about her new team and wanting to make a good impression, she would help coworkers and teammates meet deadlines on their projects. She experienced guilt about being away from her kids more often, so she signed up for activities she felt obligated to do to make up for lost time. No matter what she was doing, she worried greatly about appeasing and accommodating everyone else's expectations and demands. She would load up on energy drinks and caffeine just to get through every day. And every night, she would fall asleep with the television on, often with her phone in her hand.

Brittany was experiencing the exhaustion and depletion of a dysregulated Empath. As excited as she had been about the new promotion, it commanded a great deal of time and energy from her. She no longer had her quiet home office she could retreat to; her two-minute commute from the kitchen to her desk in the basement had become a forty-minute commute on the best of days; and the simple, consistent routine that enabled her to get out for her early morning runs was long gone. As much as she loved customer care, she was now the person they called whenever there was a problem, and she found it challenging to cope with their frustration and aggravation. She often felt hurt and overcome by those calls for several hours after the problems had been resolved.

Our work together centered around rebalancing her time and energy, establishing boundaries, and processing and managing her emotion and energy with employees and customers, especially after difficult calls. Her first step was to remember to breathe. As simple as it sounds, she recognized how often she held her breath in traffic, during a call, and all while she was at the volunteer events. She found a small nook in the stairwell at work where she could take refuge when she needed it, and she committed to walking the stairs three or four times a day to move her energy and to help release stress and strain.

Brittany incorporated a scheduling app that allowed her team members to schedule appointment times during specific office hours she would make available rather than having people stopping in and inter-rupting her work demands. She played soft music to lessen the noise and disruption and turned off the overhead lights when she could. It was quite challenging, but she committed to no electronics in her bedroom, no more energy drinks, and limited her coffee to two morning cups.

By tuning in to the emotion and energy she was experiencing and learning to give what she had, rather than what was expected of her, Brittany was finally able to manage her daily experience. And in response to that awful parental guilt, she made a commitment to herself and to her girls that she would read to them each night for fifteen minutes no matter what. Instead of taking on all those tasks and projects driven by what she felt she "should" do, she committed to quality time rather than quantity time.

As an Empath, you may not have filters or coping mechanisms when exposed to emotions and energy, so instead, you absorb them and try to acclimate yourself to the demands and expectations of others. You feel all the feels of life, even if they're not yours, and though you're capable of deep emotion, strong insight, and profound connection, you will become exhausted and depleted without the necessary tools and regulatory skills needed.

The mission of this work is to enhance your gifts, while empowering you with the wisdom and resources you need to lead life heart-centered, yet grounded, boundaried, and solid in your Sense of Self (SOS). This is the part of you that tunes inward to navigate life's tasks and decisions, the solid part of you that knows how to process and regulate through much of the adulting world as effectively as possible.

Everyone goes through life differently, and emotions and exchanges are experienced at varying levels and with distinct sensory practices that are essential for you to be in tune with, and to know how to regulate and manage. This process is extremely individualized, and only you can decide what you need in any given situation and what's in your best interest.

Plagued or pleased? Life can go either way for an Empath. Empaths can live in extremes of life and be deeply impacted by its sharp edges. Boundaries, self-care, balance, setting your pace, and healthy support systems may be foreign concepts to you. *Regulation* is the process of being conscious and in tune with your mood, behaviors, and energy, then properly reassessing and reestablishing whenever and however you need to. This practice allows you to know yourself, your strengths, your needs, and then navigate your experiences successfully.

Regulate is defined as "to fix or adjust the time, amount, degree, or rate of" by Merriam-Webster. In this context, I've defined it as the work necessary to control or maintain emotional and energetic balance and stability as you process through your day interacting with others, making decisions, having conversations, and focusing your self-care and well-being. Staying open to and grounded in your own experiences, feelings, and needs will allow you to manage yourself in relations and engagement with others, rather than getting tangled up in stressors and absorbing emotions from others.

Learning to regulate your experiences, senses, sensory input, emotion, and energy is critical for an Empath. It enhances your ability to adjust yourself and your interactions effectively and enjoyably. Saying no when you need to, knowing how to detach and move energy, leaving an environment when you want to leave, resting when you're feeling low, being around people and things you enjoy, taking time to properly refuel, and relieving the laser focus of your thoughts and feelings—these are all ways you can stabilize and remain in your solid Sense of Self.

Clearly, Empaths are sensitive. Just like someone who is greatly affected by sun exposure needs to take precaution and properly prepare, so it is for the Empath. Because you have heightened abilities for sensing, relating, connecting, and understanding people and situations, it is essential to manage your mind and mood to honor what you're experiencing and how it's impacting you. Knowing how, when, and with whom to engage and interact will allow you to adjust yourself as needed. Empaths make great friends, partners, advocates, leaders, and listeners when properly boundaried.

Everyone's process for regulation is quite personal and unique, but here are a few examples of how you can start:

- Remember to breathe. It's common to hold your breath or take shallow breaths during stress or when not grounded. Breathing moves you out of that fight/flight part of your brain.
- Physically move your body—walk, stretch, jump up and down, roll your head and shoulders.

- Practice detachment from people physically, emotionally, and/or energetically.
- Understand the different ways your mind, body, and spirit are impacted by stress, interactions, busyness, etc., and take appropriate action to care for yourself.
- Agree to things you want to do and say no to things you don't.
- Distinguish your feelings, needs, and experiences from those of others.
- Learn to recognize the difference between regulated and dysregulated so you can understand your signs and symptoms when you start to get stressed or overwhelmed.
- Make decisions that are in your best interest, regardless of others' feedback or opinion.
- Prioritize self-care.
- Assess opportunities before committing.
- Process situations and emotions as they occur so you can determine your course of action rather than allow things to accumulate.
- Know how and when to have conversations with someone when necessary and what you're hoping to accomplish in your exchange with them.
- Step away from people, places, and things that don't serve you well, temporarily, or permanently.

Regulation enables more effective decision-making as you clarify your needs and motives while considering your course of action (or nonaction). Different experiences and different people all impact you in varying ways. Be honest and aware in understanding the who, what, when, where, how, and why you're doing something (or not doing something).

What you're doing, how often you're doing it, whom you're doing it for, and why you're doing it are important points to consider as you learn to regulate yourself.

After eight years of marriage, Mary divorced David when her children were little. The marriage wasn't horrible, but she realized she had married him simply because he paid attention to her and showed up when he said he would. She liked the attention and felt bad for him, believing she would eventually learn to love him. Sadly, she never did. She carried around tremendous guilt for the ways her children were impacted by the dreaded stigma of living in two separate households and often imagined them to be forever harmed by the terrible adult choices she had made. Confusion and pity had motivated her to marry, and guilt fueled most of her parental decisions.

She called me early one Monday morning to reschedule her appointment, explaining that her kids had a field trip at school, and as much as she hated baseball, she *had* to sign up to chaperone each of the children separately. As a matter of fact, she felt it her duty to tag along at every outing the kids had, served as the room mom for the third year in a row, and volunteered at school events, including plays, musicals, making copies, bake sales, etc. Guilt served as the undercurrent of most of what she did.

My return call offered her a personal challenge rather than the different appointment time she'd been looking for. The challenge suggested she could skip the baseball trips this time around. Maybe these opportunities could be extended to another parent who did indeed love the sport and would have fun creating that memory with their child, and she could instead commit to picking the kids up and taking them for ice cream so they could share about their experience at the ballpark.

Mary considered the offer but couldn't quite embrace the challenge. She did, however, start with smaller steps and allowed several upcoming volunteer opportunities to pass by without signing up. The guilt was incredible at first, but after she sat with it long enough and allowed those feelings to surface, she realized how much sadness and grief she still had about the divorce—not because she wanted to reunite with David but because she simply didn't want to have a divided family. Dealing with her grief allowed her to make decisions that made her feel good about the interactions she had with her kids rather than reacting out of the pain of grief and guilt.

Compare empathy to a trait such as generosity. It is a beautiful quality to have, and a little can go a long way. It can be helpful, even life changing in certain circumstances. Yet, if you overextend, give more than you can afford, or don't leave a reserve for yourself, you can experience big trouble. If you are so generous that you give away your mortgage payment, you'll create problems for yourself. So too, if you're over-functioning, unboundaried, unaware, and misusing your empathy and kindness while not realizing what's driving your moods and behaviors, it will be harmful and counterproductive.

It's imperative for Empaths not to mistake codependency for kindness and overextend their empathic abilities, but to properly "budget" their time, effort, and energy so they don't wind up overdrawn or emotionally bankrupt. Spending time with people you want to spend time with, going places you want to go, doing things you want to do, having healthy support and coping, offering compassion and support to people when you have it to give, maintaining a healthy schedule and routine—these are all ways you can practice and enhance regulation. Awareness, boundaries, self-care, and personal responsibility are tools that help you make decisions and act in your best interest to care for yourself as needed.

WHAT IS DYSREGULATION?

Bryan could hardly contain himself as he sat in afternoon traffic. He'd been trying to be nice by doing a favor for a neighbor. He could feel the heat rise into his neck and his shoulders tense as his heart rate pulsed. He was late to drop off the papers his neighbor asked him to take care of while he was out—seven minutes late and still miles to travel, yet traffic held still. Despite rushing, people were left waiting for him, and he couldn't bear the thought of being late and disappointing someone.

His fingers turned red from the solid grip on the steering wheel, and as he saw the clock turn to 3:08, he suddenly pounded on the horn. The blast of noise surprised even him, yet he couldn't seem to let off the horn. What kind of solution would that bring to the hundreds of cars surrounding him?

"Why does this always happen when I'm in a hurry?" he barked at the invisible passenger next to him. "It serves me right for trying to be Mr. Nice Guy."

Since he'd already let loose, he gave the horn another frustrated punch, trying to move the traffic gridlocked in front of him.

His thoughts flooded, his pulse rose, and his head began to ache. "Never again will I do something nice for someone. Never again will I waste time for people. Stuff like this happens all the time. Never again!"

Bryan knew he was out of control, but he had no idea how to reel it in and calm himself down.

As an Empath, you've likely heard phrases such as:

- "What's the big deal? Why can't you just relax?"
- "What in the world is wrong with you?"
- "Why are you overreacting?"

- "Have you seen your doctor? Maybe you should take some medicine."
- "You need to take a chill pill."
- "Why are you always so extreme?"
- "You're always so stressed out."

An Empath's reactions can be strong and seemingly out of proportion with the circumstance. You have big feelings and perceive things on deep levels, so it's easy to become overwhelmed or to allegedly overreact. Seemingly small things like rushing, hurriedness, what others may think or feel, overstimulation, chaos, or noise can add a great deal of intensity to your moods and reactions. You can get out of whack and feel derailed by common experiences, interactions, and events when you don't have proper awareness and aren't managing yourself and stressors properly.

Dysregulation is defined as "abnormality or impairment in the regulation of a metabolic, physiological, or psychological process" by Oxford Languages. You may slip into this state quickly and easily without recognizing what's happening. It's as though an invisible scale tips, and suddenly you're drained, fed up, finished, and perhaps even furious. You are especially at risk of this when you're not taking care of yourself, maintaining your boundaries, or managing your energy and emotions effectively.

Essentially, it can be challenging to understand and handle your emotional responses and the stress of interacting with others. As a big feeler who doesn't always recognize how to process experiences, your systems and reactions can get seriously out of whack.

Dysregulation can be caused by the following:

- People-pleasing and lack of Sense of Self (SOS)
- Lack of attunement and awareness

- Outward focus rather than internal
- Not listening to or honoring your feelings, needs, and physical cues
- Absorbing the emotions and energy of others
- Overextending, over-functioning
- Lack of boundaries
- Overcommitting—busyness, distraction, loss of priorities
- Self-neglect and poor self-care
- Focusing on someone else's needs more than your own
- Destructive self-talk and mental chatter
- Laughing at something you find hurtful
- Giving time, energy, or effort you don't have to give

Think about it. If you become saturated with stress and emotion, give away energy you don't have, take on issues that aren't yours, over-function, and make yourself available in ways and times that aren't good for you, there will be dysregulation somewhere in your life.

Dysregulation often comes out sideways and can be experienced in ways such as these:

- Reactions that seem extreme and out of proportion with the situation
- Rigidity and extremes—absolutes, all-or-none, black-and-white thinking
- Exhaustion, irritability, depletion
- Sleep disturbance
- Addiction—food, substances, shopping, etc.
- Shutting down, isolation, inability to function
- Somatic issues and illness
- Mood disturbances

- Hyperfocus, obsession, excessive activity, and busyness
- Attempts to manage and control

WATCH YOURSELF

You can't pour from an empty cup. As a dysregulated or disempowered Empath, you can present risks and dysfunction to yourself and others. You may become saturated with other people's emotion, pain, stress, and struggles. If you're not conscious and deliberate about taking care of yourself, you're at risk of self-destructive, codependent ways of relating. Taking on the emotions and experiences of those around you can lead to a multitude of physical, emotional, financial, spiritual, occupational, and relational issues. Not knowing how to manage your experiences, detach, or move energy is likely to exhaust and deplete you.

Further, if you overextend yourself in any capacity over long periods of time, you're likely to attract a whole community of people who benefit from your caretaking behaviors. You, on the other hand, will be struggling and suffering. Lack of awareness, people-pleasing, overcommitting, and codependency are not kind. They are signs of unhealthy relationship patterns.

As a deep feeler and tenderhearted soul, you probably see the potential in others and invest heavily in trying to develop that potential, even to your own detriment. Continual acts of kindness and consideration can go too far when you aren't aware of what you're doing and why you're doing it, aren't managing your energy and emotion well, or aren't being honest about your patterns of relating.

It's common for unaware Empaths to have significant health problems because of the stress and strain of all of this. When you're overly attuned to the feelings and needs of others and aren't so mindful of your own, it's only a matter of time before the body begins to show signs and symptoms of that wear and tear.

Your body is the vehicle you've been granted to support and sustain you. Dysfunction and dysregulation are damaging and stressful to the body and mind. Depleting patterns of coping and relating will eventually take their toll. Just like the proper care and maintenance of an automobile, lawn, or bank account, you have that same personal responsibility to your well-being. There's a rudimentary level of attention, self-care, and upkeep you need to engage in to ensure your personal safety and well-being.

Think of the illustration of water. It needs to be able to move and flow, and when it can't do so effectively, it will press against the barriers until they eventually burst. The same is true for emotion and energy. When these are obstructed, clogged, or blocked, the body will develop signs of stress and strain. Somatic symptoms such as gastrointestinal issues, headaches, muscle aches, unexplained aches and pains, sleep disturbance, weight issues, etc. are cries for help. They are all ways the body may be storing the energy and emotion and trying to regulate against dysfunction.

You experience mental, physical, and emotional energy, and it is constantly flowing through the body whether you're conscious of it or not. It is critical to pay attention to the way you feel and what the body is trying to communicate. Fatigue is a cry for rest. Sleep disturbance is likely a cry for some type of release or reflection, something that needs your attention. Tightness and strain in your neck and shoulders is evidence of stress, need for release, or movement. What are your signs and symptoms trying to communicate to you?

How you take in energy and emotion and the ways these affect your body will give you evidence of what you need to regulate yourself, how you can manage your mood and energy properly, and how you can move or dispel energy when you need to. Ignoring, suppressing, denying, and shaming the ways you feel are dangerous and destructive acts that will eventually cause complications.

SPECIAL CARE AND CONSIDERATION

Experiencing the heavy weight of emotion the way you do can be riddling, and without awareness and effective coping mechanisms you'll be left relying on destructive methods to soothe and regulate yourself. Empaths often resort to numbing and distracting themselves from the intensity of life. Overwhelm and overstimulation, coupled with the inability to filter, regulate, or protect yourself from these multisensory experiences, will leave you susceptible to high levels of dysfunction. The use of alcohol, substances, busyness, self-harm, exercise, shopping, food, and sex can be anesthetizing. You may find yourself at the extremes of overindulging or neglecting your needs or desires without knowing how to pace or sustain yourself.

The statistics are not clear or well-documented, but from my perspective, the number of dysregulated or at-risk Empaths is shocking. Lack of knowledge and awareness of how to process what you're experiencing, along with dysfunctional patterns of relating, leaves you plagued by emotion and energy and consumed by the intensity of it all. Feelings of sadness, irritability, exhaustion, and anxiety, along with rapidly shifting moods, impulsivity, isolation, lability, and instability, can be too much to know how to deal with.

The concern is that these symptoms also mimic multiple mental health diagnoses. Though medication has its necessary time and purpose, misdiagnosing and medicating a dysregulated Empath is tragic and disempowering. It misses the point, breeds misinformation, and treats the symptoms rather than educating and empowering the Empath to understand what's happening within them and how to use their gifts for good. Treating professionals, loved ones, Empaths, and the world at large would be much better served with proper information, resources, skills, and coping strategies.

Years ago, we believed the world was flat, that crying kids were best served by letting them cry it out, and that kids who struggled in school were lazy or bad. Education and experimentation have expanded and corrected our understanding and reshaped how we see things. So too with the understanding of an Empath—not someone who is crazy, dysfunctional, too much, mentally ill, or ill wired. Simply someone who needs to be properly educated and equipped for dealing and coping with emotion, energy, exchanges, and environment.

Before we proceed, let's do the proper disclaimer: I am *NOT* recommending that you stop any meds you've been prescribed. That is a very personal issue, one best determined between you and your doctor. I am simply offering insight into the importance of proper education and awareness for Empaths and diagnosing professionals. Education is a way to gain knowledge and understanding to move into a place of empowerment and healthy awareness.

That education begins by turning the search inward and asking yourself a few key questions . . .

✿ REFLECTION QUESTIONS

....

*God has given each of you a gift from his great
variety of spiritual gifts.*

Use them well to serve one another.

—1 PETER 4:10, NEW LIVING TRANSLATION

....

I recognize myself as a regulated Empath:

☐ NOT AT ALL   ☐ SOMEWHAT   ☐ A GREAT DEAL

Some of my dysregulated tendencies include the following:

1.

2.

3.

I tend to overextend myself in the following ways:

1.

2.

3.

I invest in others' potential rather than seeing people and situations
as they are:

☐ NOT AT ALL   ☐ SOMEWHAT   ☐ A GREAT DEAL

Unhealthy coping and relating patterns I recognize in myself:

1.

2.

3.

I've experienced the world to be: (stressful, unkind, scary, safe, amazing, an opportunity).

1.

2.

3.

As an Empath, I recognize my strengths and gifts as these:

1.

2.

3.

PERSONAL LEARNING:

CHAPTER 2

The Emotions of an Empath

Let's not forget that the little emotions are the great captains of our lives, and we obey them without realizing it.

—VINCENT VAN GOGH

Tammy burst into my office from the reception area without waiting for my wave to invite her in. Her energy seemed pressured, frantic almost, as she took a seat on the couch and poured out a story she needed to tell. She had been working at a local school for many years, and recently, they hired a new aide. He was nice enough, smiled, made eye contact, and always followed through with tasks he was assigned. But six weeks into the new arrangement, Tammy could sense that something wasn't right.

She found herself watching this man more closely and detecting small things he would do to position himself strategically at the lunch tables of the younger children. She noticed when he sat a little too closely to one of the kids or patted their hand as he gave a few of them an extra fifty cents for ice cream. The hair on the back of her neck stood up every time he walked into the room. As a matter of fact, she remembered an anxious, sinking feeling the very first time she met him. It was a feeling she had dismissed, accusing herself of being snarky. But the truth was that she *knew* something was wrong. She could feel it, even though nothing had *actually* happened.

I spent most of the session acknowledging and validating her experience and educating her on the importance and legitimacy of emotions like these. We talked about the essential gut-level knowing that most people have, an innate sense that our feelings are trying to awaken and enlighten us about something that we can't immediately see with our eyes. It took Tammy some time to understand and accept the power of those feelings, but once she did, she moved easily into a solution to meet with her principal the next day after she documented specific details that triggered those senses inside her.

Think of emotion as energy in motion. Framed in this way, any emotion (or energy) you're feeling offers information and insight that is worth your attention. Just as the body will speak through pain, an ache, or numbness, so too does emotion leave traces of evidence for you to investigate. Despite popular belief, there are no right or wrong feelings; all feelings are just cues and sources of information that compel you to inquire within yourself.

Most people aren't cognizant of what's happening inside them and have a hard time determining their feelings. Further, some people hold a lot of judgment of certain emotions they experience and struggle to acknowledge them. Certain emotions like stress, jealousy, confusion, or dread may be misinterpreted as a character flaw, a weakness, or somehow bad.

You might not be conscious of what emotion you're experiencing, or it may be so minor and obscure that you don't recognize it, but make no mistake, there is never a time when you are totally without an emotion.

Though you may not understand what you're feeling, I assure you, the emotion is there.

Your emotions reveal an immediate sense about a person, place, or situation. This "immediate sense"—or "vibe," if you will—is not something to be dismissed; it is important information. Just like you would take time to feel your way through a dark room, your emotions can innately lead and direct you through situations. They are intuitive sources that enlighten you to different levels of information, but only if you think about them as data worth investigating.

What was that sense of dread when you pulled into the parking lot? Why did you experience that discomfort when your boss closed the office door? Why were you compelled to drive a different way home than you normally go? Why are you suddenly anxious? What happened to cause your energy to just drop?

There are no concrete measurements we can apply to these experiences, and yet they are all credible indicators worth investigating. It is your responsibility to tune in and honor what your feelings are trying to communicate to you. They want to tell you something. Are you listening?

THE NEW F-WORD

Feelings get a bad rap. They're terribly misrepresented, often dismissed as overdramatic and senseless. As an Empath who experiences big feelings, there's a great chance that this mishandling has led to a lot of confusion and distortion about you and your emotions. It's possible that others have compounded this dilemma by discrediting, chastising, or making fun of your feelings. One of the driving forces in life—the way you feel—has likely been held against you in some way, whether by others or by yourself.

Most people, even young children, have some basic knowledge of general emotions like "mad," "sad," and "glad." Those can be a good starting point, but there's usually a lot more to it. Emotions can be complex and multilayered, with depth and nuance to processing and regulating them. It's one thing to detect a feeling, but it's an entirely different level of awareness to know what to do with it when it arises.

Imagine being in a room filled with the sounds of dozens of voices, all different volumes, and tones. You can clearly hear them, but you can't determine what they're saying, who's saying what, or even where they're coming from. Now imagine living in that room every day. It would be maddening, wouldn't it? The emotional experience of an Empath can feel very much the same.

Are you flooded by emotions and sensory experiences you can't seem to understand? Are there things you can detect but can't really tell what they are or if they're coming from inside you or somewhere else? How easily do you understand what these cues are trying to tell you? Once you do recognize them, do you know what to do with them? Most people don't have any idea how to answer these questions, and it can lead to serious problems. For an Empath, it can be even worse.

Irritability, anxiety, discomfort, worry, angst, uncertainty, frustration, confusion, anger, and hurt are all legitimate emotions. Consider them to be a knock at the door, requesting your attention and investigation. If someone knocks at the door, you don't hide under the bed, jump out the window, or draw your guns to start shooting. Hopefully, you don't ignore or deny the knock either. Likewise, you don't blindly open up and holler, "Come on in." A knock simply requires inquiry and exploration. So it is with your feelings. They are messages and pieces of information for you to assess and examine as you determine what's going on and what the emotional "knock" on your door is trying to communicate to you.

With all this in mind, it is also important to remember that feelings are not *fact*. Neither are they always the best decision-makers, especially for Empaths who feel so much. They are, however, handled most effectively when you take the time and care to examine and explore the message they're trying to deliver. The more you familiarize yourself with the plethora of emotions and how your body responds to them, the more you will be able to detect and decipher the specific messages and details your feelings want you to know.

GO WITH YOUR GUT

Have you heard the phrase "two minds are better than one"? Well, do I have good news for you!

There is magnificent power in the mind, so imagine what life could be like with the support and guidance of two brains. In addition to the brain you're already aware of, researchers have started to understand the gut to be the second brain. The "brain" in your belly directly communicates information and feedback to the brain in your head and vice versa. One is very analytical, and the other is instinctual and intuitive. Comprised of almost thirty feet of one hundred million neurons, the gut's capabilities for deciphering information and dictating physical and emotional health is just as significant as the brain's.[3]

---

3   Hadhazy, Adam. "Think Twice: How the Gut's "Second Brain" Influences Mood and Well-Being." Scientific American. February 12, 2010.

Have you ever heard something about someone and secretly confirmed to yourself, "I knew it!"? Or were you instantly turned off by the "perfect date" your coworker set you up on, only to find out later that she had a longstanding history of adultery? Or, after a third interview with a prime, up-and-coming company, you refused their offer because something felt uncomfortable, despite the promising salary and benefit package, only to hear about their disbanding six months later? A hunch, a knowing, a gut feeling, a premonition—these are all intuitive ways the body knows and can detect various things in the world.

It's likely you have some type of Spidey-senses that alert you to cues and intuitive information despite how things appear, despite the "evidence" in front of you, or despite other people's endorsements. Empaths often just *know* something, often without details, evidence, or proof. They know it in their heart and gut. You may be able to sense danger, unhealthy people, bad decisions, lies, or manipulation when no one else can. Your feelings will alert you to risk, distress, or opportunities that are not right for you. It is critical to honor what these senses are telling you.

Just as you've expanded your intelligence and wisdom over the years, it's also possible to improve your gut sense. Practical tools such as awareness and inquiry will allow you to develop the trust necessary to relax into and get curious about emotions as they surface. A silly example perhaps, but think of a turtle. When this creature is allowed its own time, pace, and readiness, it will come out of its shell and mosey along. The same is true for the messages of the gut. As you witness and allow intuitive information to emerge without trying to probe, force, manipulate, suppress, deny, or minimize it, your intuition will offer information, insight, and perspective that you may have otherwise missed or overlooked.

Feelings and intuition only create problems when they're not listened to or properly dealt with. When you allow yourself to contemplate and inquire about an opportunity, decision, or person, the body will perceive and offer information that the mind may miss or override. You will instinctively *know* an answer or have a sense if you learn to tune in and recognize what your gut is offering. Allow yourself to *feel* into something as an empowering way to use your emotions and gut sense in conjunction with the logic and reasoning of your brain.

ENERGETIC EXCHANGE

Everything is energy. Like air, you can breathe in the energy around you even though you can't see it. You're affected by the quality of it. You may absorb the energy, emotions, and moods of others, and be impacted by different environments and the exchanges you have. Because you're so influenced and impacted by what's happening around you, it's critical to assess the health and quality of your interactions with people, places, and things. Their energy can take on many different forms and can set the tone for your entire day if you're not conscious of what's happening.

Relating to anything or anyone is an energetic exchange. Some are far more positive than others. Some are more impactful than others. A conversation, an interaction at the grocery store, a traffic altercation, walking by someone, sitting in a meeting, having dinner, taking a trip, a physical touch, buying something, starting a relationship, ending a relationship—all are examples of an energetic exchange. These exchanges may be rewarding and fulfilling to you. They also may be exhausting, depleting, or far too much for you at any given point.

45

Why is this? As an Empath, you not only feel your own energy, but also that of others. Energy can be contaminating and contagious if you don't practice methods of managing and regulating yourself very much like "energetic hygiene." Your energy can be fine until you have an exchange with someone, sit next to them at an appointment, or listen to them talk about their neighbor's cousin who you don't know. Suddenly, you feel differently, and you may not even know why. You've caught an energetic bug you weren't aware of.

Your first step is *noticing*. When did your energy shift? What are you feeling, and what do you need to do to manage it? How are you feeling as you engage or partake in any exchange? Is it possible to get yourself grounded? What's the driving force behind the decision you're making? Are the emotions and sensations you're experiencing your own or could they belong to someone else?

Energy has different intensities and vibrations to it. Have you ever met someone and found them to be abrasive without them saying a word? Have you ever walked into a place and instantly gone on high alert and felt your senses become bombarded? Those sensations are energy, and it's highly impactful to your mind, body, and spirit. If not recognized and managed, it can alter your mood and engagement without understanding what's happening.

When you're experiencing something that's heavy, dark, overwhelming, and burdensome, you may have a hard time shaking it off or getting out from underneath the weight of it. Energy can be moved, shifted, and deflected to help you detach from it and move it through or away from you. Learning to experiment with different techniques and practices will allow you to regulate emotion more easily and improve your mood and engagement with others as you lighten and loosen the heaviness of different situations and interactions.

As you learn to maneuver energy differently, visualization can be a fun, creative practice. Picturing energy as a ball of light with various textures, sizes, colors, and temperatures can be helpful as you learn to recognize what energy feels like, understand what to do with it, and determine how to manage it effectively. If you're in a challenging situation or feeling irritated or overwhelmed, you can use imagery and imagination to shift, move, and shrink the energy to creatively lessen it or move it out of your personal experience. Just like something you might wipe off of you or gently push away from you, so too can you visualize doing this with energy. With practice, you can learn to ride the wave of good-feeling vibes, as well as move negative energy out and through you so you're not plagued by it. You can learn different methods to focus and magnify the intensity and longevity of positive energy, as well as dispel remnants of negative energy.

We'll talk more about ways to move and play with energy fields.

SCALE OF EMOTION

Below is a Scale of Emotion that illustrates the energetic continuum of a multitude of feelings. This scale is based on the work of Esther and Jerry Hicks, who offer practical tools of emotional and energetic management and regulation.[4] The bottom of the scale reflects deeper, heavier emotion, and as you work your way up the scale, you will recognize the subtle shifts that lighten the weight of the emotion. None of these are right or wrong, good or bad. They are simply emotional states that are important for you to be aware of as you engage in different energetic practices.

---

4   *The Astonishing Power of Emotions* by Esther and Jerry Hicks. Hay House Inc. 2007.

1. Joy / Appreciation / Love / Freedom
2. Empowerment
3. Passion
4. Enthusiasm / Eagerness
5. Happiness
6. Positive Belief or Expectation
7. Hopefulness
8. Optimism
9. Curiousness
10. Contentment
11. Boredom
12. Pessimism / Doubt
13. Frustration / Irritation / Impatience
14. Discouragement / Dismay / Disheartenment
15. Overwhelm
16. Disappointment
17. Worry
18. Blame
19. Anger
20. Revenge
21. Hatred / Rage
22. Jealousy
23. Guilt
24. Insecurity / Unworthiness
25. Shame
26. Grief
27. Depression / Despair
28. Fear / Powerlessness

We've all experienced emotion somewhere along this range, and we have all likely felt stuck on one level or another. You are allowed to feel any emotion you need to, for as long as you need to. And it's important to know what you focus on magnifies, so it is critical not to stay or wallow too long in the low-riding vibes or fuel them with negativity and fear. Doing so creates the risk of those emotions becoming a chronic state or outlook. The more you practice an emotion or trained thought, the more momentum it gains, and before you know it, it becomes an avalanche.

Lingering in any of the low-energy vibes will impact your mood, perspective, thoughts, and behaviors. You cannot force yourself through an emotion, but you can practice small energetic shifts or boosts to try to loosen or lighten it. You are not wrong to feel anything that you need to, and it's important to process through, regulate, and soothe as soon and as much as you can. The goal of this work is awareness and improving your ability to shift your energy and attention subtly yet deliberately up the scale.

You can learn to move, process, and shift emotion, and you will become more skilled at it the more you practice. If you've ever driven a manual vehicle, you know that shifting from one gear to another is a repetitious training that requires patience and focus. Trying to move too quickly from first to fifth gear without the proper strategic maneuvering is too drastic of a shift and will not work. However, with some well-practiced manipulation, you can smoothly and efficiently move from first to second, second to third, and so on until you're up to speed. So it is with the energetic scale.

An attempt to climb from grief to joy is too big of a leap, one that will perpetuate low-energy emotion such as frustration, despair, or anger. If something has just happened or there is an intense amount of emotion you're experiencing, then small, gentle shifts are necessary to move the needle up the scale. Moving from hatred to anger may not feel like much progress, but energetically, it is—and it is also far more realistic and manageable a shift. From anger, you can assess the next shift you're ready to make.

You walk into the office one Monday morning to discover the president of the company standing at your desk. He goes on and on about budget cuts, quarterly numbers, and necessary changes, and at the end of it all, you're left with the harsh reality that you've just lost your job after years of hard work and dedication. You're flooded with shock, anger, devastation, fury, rage, embarrassment, and fear. These are all natural emotions reflecting a devastating situation, and you're likely to feel those for a while.

Your journey out of the depths of these emotions is a matter of taking incremental steps and small shifts. As you practice this work, you start by determining your lowest level on the Scale of Emotion. At first you think it's anger. After all, you've given a lot of blood, sweat, and tears for that place, and they fired you. Yet, you know as you sit with the emotion, it's deeper than that. When you really tune in and learn to listen to the emotion, you recognize it as fear. Fear of what others will think, of starting over, going into debt, and suddenly the fears begin to mount. You breathe, giving yourself a little room and permission to feel that without collapsing under the weight of the emotional flood and mental entourage.

Knowing that both anger and fear are normal reactions to the situation and having stabilized yourself a bit with breath and perspective, the next step is to look for emotions higher up the scale that you can settle into. Small shifts or thought and self-talk that include something like these:

- "Well, at least I don't have to give that ridiculous presentation next week." (Optimism)
- "I have six months' severance and enough savings to cover me for six more. I know I'll figure something out." (Contentment)

If shifting to such positive emotions proves too challenging at first, then think about a smaller shift like this:

- "I gave years of my life to a company that never appreciated me, saw my value, or used me to my potential. But I got a master's degree on their dime." (Revenge, though still a heavy energy, is still higher on the scale than fear.)

It can take time to settle into a higher frequency when things seem so devastating. Don't force it or pretend to feel something you don't. Fake it till you make it doesn't always work too well with energy. Those Spidey-senses know the truth about how you feel. Shifting, soothing, and breathing through difficult emotions is how you move through them, not shaming, denying, suppressing, or pretending.

This scale gives you an entire menu of emotions to choose from. Meet yourself exactly where you are, and gently and consistently move yourself up the scale as steadily as you can. Take small, consistent steps to work your way up the scale by focusing your thoughts, attention, and perspective to align with different feelings until you find one that feels manageable.

You can't force a shift, but you can take your eyes off a problem for a moment and focus on something simple that allows less intensity and heaviness. You can concentrate on a word that's inspiring (*possibility*, *love*, *hope*). Repeat it over and over again and practice feeling it in your body.

Look at a picture that sparks a smile. Imagine yourself in the picture or recall the memories or people presented in the photo. Ask Siri to tell you a knock-knock joke. Call someone you love. Even momentary relief from heavy emotion is progress.

Small modifications simply move you up the scale. You don't have to move into joy and appreciation right away. It may take you a long time to realize why that crummy old job needed to go and accept that they did you a favor by firing you because you weren't happy but never would've left on your own. Take your time with this practice and be deliberate and intentional about the thoughts you use that fuel your feelings.

EMOTIONAL INTELLIGENCE

Emotional Intelligence is a way of recognizing, understanding, and choosing how we think, feel, and act. It shapes our interactions with others and our understanding of ourselves. It defines how and what we learn; it allows us to set priorities; it determines the majority of our daily actions. Research suggests it is responsible for as much as 80 percent of the "success" in our lives.

—JOSHUA FREEDMAN

Emotional Intelligence (EI) is not a term I love to introduce to my clients. When I asked Siri what the opposite of intelligence is, she answered, "Stupidity." See my dilemma? Yet EI is perhaps one of the most important factors when it comes to relating, coping, decision-making, and problem-solving. It is the ability to recognize, understand, and process your emotions while being able to do the same with the emotions of others.

Because the emotions of an Empath can be complex and profound, you certainly may feel stupid, incapable, foolish, or insane whenever they become overwhelming. Being an Empath does not guarantee that you have Emotional Intelligence. As a matter of fact, many Empaths are riddled and bombarded with the ways they experience the world and can benefit greatly from proper tools and techniques for processing emotions effectively. It is imperative for Empaths to develop skills of discernment and regulation in identifying how their emotional experience differs from those around them. There is skill, art, and finesse associated with emotional management, and you can become quite skilled at it the more you recognize and accept the emotions you experience.

It starts by acknowledging that energy, emotion, thought, and behavior influence one another. Learn to name an emotion so you can tune in to the thought patterns that fuel your thoughts and behaviors. Does disappointment automatically trigger thoughts of defeat, causing you to shut down and withdraw? Do hurt feelings propel you into passive-aggressive behaviors because you don't know how to use words to express yourself? Does the fear of failure or embarrassment keep you from saying yes to opportunities and keep you playing small in life? Does the discomfort of conflict have you stuck in a relationship that isn't good for you because you dread the possibility of someone being upset, or worse, being alone? Does the anger and intensity of your boss keep you in a role of people-pleasing and over-functioning because you can't bear his energy?

Because feelings and thoughts fuel one another and drive your behavior, they create a perpetual cycle of success or struggle. Which path are you consistently choosing? Practiced patterns become habitual and set the foundation for how you think, cope, connect, and interact in the world.

They shape your beliefs about yourself and others, and the longer you entertain them, the more solidified they become and the stronger they will influence all parts of your life. Developing methods to recognize, soothe, and regulate each of these is critical to your well-being. Awareness is your starting point. Then, you're able to understand how you've used certain behavior and patterns to cope and function. Offer your mind something positive to feel into and concentrate on every day as often as you can to provide it with a focal grounding point. Allow that to become your well-practiced, habitual thought. This is the beginning of EI, grounding, and regulation. It is not a cure; it is a practice.

COMMODITIES

EMOTION—*a natural instinctive state of mind deriving from one's circumstances, mood, or relationships with others; instinctive or intuitive feeling as distinguished from reasoning or knowledge.*

—OXFORD LANGUAGES

Natural, instinctive, intuitive—these are words used to define and support the validity of the emotions you experience. These physical and emotional indicators are intended to serve as cues and signs for your senses and systems. Your body always knows, and it will speak to you, and it is your responsibility to listen closely.

Like a trusted fuel light that comes on when gas is running low or a bank alert that announces when an account is dangerously low, emotions serve as internal cues indicating that you are also depleted in some capacity. Taking these cues into consideration will allow you to stay awake, alert, and alive at the wheel of your life.

Though we live in a society that seems to prioritize wealth and accumulation, I have found there are three primary commodities that far greater shape the health and quality of your life. The precious commodities of time, energy, and effort matter greatly, and the ways you spend these commodities will shape the conditions of your life.

Learning to work in conjunction with your emotions, to tune in to how something feels or the energy it commands, will alert you when something isn't right, when you're misspending or overspending any of these commodities.

It's important to remember that your gas light doesn't come on for no reason. Nor do feelings get inadvertently activated. Your feelings are accurate measures of your "spending behavior" when it comes to how you are spending your time, energy, and effort.

Time—Sixty minutes in each hour; 1,440 minutes in each day; twenty-four hours in every day; 525,949 minutes each year. How are you spending your minutes, hours, and days? Time, by far the most valuable commodity, because once you spend it, you can never get it back. The ways you invest your time will fundamentally shape the quality of your life.

Energy—This is the mental and emotional space you allow people, places, and things to occupy in your mind and heart. This includes all the mental and emotional pieces you carry for the household, work, children, partner, family members, others, and various tasks or responsibilities. What do you allow to occupy your mind? Do you step into other people's lives or take on tasks that are not yours to manage, often feeling you have "no choice"? What do you allow to live rent-free in your mind and heart? Do you stop to assess the mental and emotional capacity you have for someone or something before you engage? Do you consider the toll something takes prior to committing?

Effort—This includes the lengths you go to for someone or something, for what period of time, how often, and for what reasons? What are the tasks, habits, roles, behaviors, and responsibilities you take on and why?

At forty-two years old, Saundra struggled with what had always been a complicated relationship with her father. She loved him but found herself irritated and disappointed most of the times she visited. She went to great lengths to please him, and she always felt terribly guilty about living two hours away, leaving him alone during the week. To try to appease him and manage the guilt, she committed to weekend trips to help with cooking, cleaning, and spending time together. Every Sunday, she made the long trek back to her home, exhausted, hurt, and defeated.

The two-hour commute afforded her the opportunity to process and stew over their interactions and conversations. The replay conjured up further hurt as she focused on the level of sacrifice she was making for him. Her time, energy, and effort were being spent in ways that depleted her, and to make matters worse, her father was often angry, complaining, and bitter. Her efforts were exhausting, seemingly ineffective, and completely unappreciated. She found herself suffering from the combination of the long drive back, disgust about the filth and odor of her father's home, and the pain that came from the criticism and emotional assault he projected onto her. The constant blare of the news he insisted on watching took a further toll as well.

On one recent drive back, she kept replaying the way he swatted at her when she tried to help steady his walk. He had criticized her cooking and the way she dressed. The meals she prepped, cooked, and packaged for him would go untouched until she returned the next week. Defeated and worn-out, she questioned, "Why am I doing all of this?"

Saundra poured out her desperation in my office, and when I inquired about what her feelings might be trying to tell her, she launched into her own personal assault about what a terrible daughter she was for not being more understanding and supportive of a father with lifelong patterns of criticism and abuse. Her thoughts and words centered around what more she could do to help him. Spending more time, energy, and effort, doing more, and being more thoughtful and considerate were her only solutions to this dilemma.

I introduced her to the commodities of time, energy, and effort, and the powerful insight that emotions offer when we tune in to them. Assessing her weekly expenditure of her commodities was an eye-opener for her as she started to see the "cost" of her efforts. Of course, her expenditures had nothing to do with money. The real price came in the form of the endless hours she was spending in an overwhelming, negative, and critical environment, along with the unceasing efforts to please and care for her father, all to no avail. She had some hard decisions to make, but she was determined that her new focus would be on the importance and relevance of feelings, rather than fueling self-criticism, shame, judgment, ridicule, or suppression.

Saundra used her emotions as cues to determine how much she had to "spend" on specific tasks for her father. She looked into local support agencies and recruited help from some of his church members rather than trying to do all the work herself. Occasionally she turned the trip into a mini vacation by booking a room just outside of town so she wouldn't be immersed in his environment. She scheduled regular self-care appointments right after her weekends with him and used the drive time to debrief, breathe, and listen to something enjoyable.

At times, she let herself cry the entire way home, but the tears were different. She felt the sadness and pain of the situation and the history with this difficult man rather than the shame and pressure to do more and be more. She allowed herself to grieve the reality of all the things she would never get from the man she called "father" and the love and connection she was never able to receive.

The motive of her efforts was also different. She was no longer driven to please; she was simply offering what she could to a man who would never be able to appreciate her efforts. She was doing it because of a personal decision about who she wanted to be in the world. Though she did change some of her behaviors, most of the changes happened within her own mind and heart.

Craig made more money than he ever thought he could. He won awards, went on trips, and had experiences most people could never dream of. Yet, every day, he went to a job that ate away at his soul. His employer supported profit over people. Studies were altered, information was distorted, and Craig felt forced to promote a product he knew was not good for people. He was never home, his wife and children were sad and lonely, and he went places and did things he morally didn't agree with to gain customers, accolades, and approval. At the end of the day, he knew his time, energy, and efforts were making the rich richer while doing a disservice to the customers he had come to know and care about.

Though he was well compensated, Craig felt miserable. He was depressed, irritable, and lethargic. He had recently started gaining weight, and he found himself snapping at his children frequently, and in a way he never had before. He ridiculed himself daily, upped his workout routine to shed the weight and try to manage the frustration, and donated more money to a charity because of his "selfish" attitude, trying to redeem some sense of being a good human. His self-punishment was evident, and it was not fixing the problem, only perpetuating it. He was trying to throw solutions at things that were not the problem.

Craig was out of alignment with not only his feelings but also his values. Every time he felt something, he denied, suppressed, or judged it. He tried to be better, work harder, and give more to assuage his emotions. It seemed he was working himself into an early grave.

My sessions with Craig focused on emotional awareness and acceptance as he reestablished his priorities and values. He had never learned to inquire about his feelings, much less respect them as important information. This awareness awakened him to the realization that he had succumbed to the golden handcuffs of wealth and prestige, believing that money could override morals and quality time. He was terribly misaligned with what mattered most to him.

Craig committed to reassessing his commodities, starting small and working his way up to the ultimate decision to leave the company. It was terrifying and yet necessary. His determination was powerful as he learned to take hold of the key to his own restraints and set himself free.

Have you ever assessed the ways you're spending your commodities? Have you clarified the amount of time, energy, and effort you're spending on specific people, places, and things? What's the quality of each of these? Taking the time necessary for this assessment will offer great insight into your patterns, habits, and well-being. Like Saundra and Craig, you may be awakened to what your mind, body, and heart have been trying to tell you. Each of these parts offers important information and cues when you learn to tune in, honor, and align with what's in your best interest.

Your time, energy, and effort are treasured resources. It is your responsibility to effectively manage them to the best of your ability. Use your emotions as a guide for how to spend these resources in ways that will best support and sustain you.

Important note—changing the ways you interact with others and your lifelong patterns is not an easy, simple process. There can be a lot of turmoil, upset, and uncertainty to this work and establishing the necessary changes. People are accustomed to specific roles and responsibilities you've carried and changing those may evoke serious disruption. Utilizing the tools and resources associated with this process of Enlightenment allows you to stay the course, but it does not always make it easy.

As a final reflection, consider the following questions:

- When something's wrong, how does your body speak to you?
- What emotions do you experience when you've overspent your time, energy, or effort?
- Where are you overspending (people, places, and things)?
- Why are you doing this? (Take some time to really consider your motives. Be honest with yourself.)
- What is the impact (emotional, mental, physical, moral) of this overspending?
- What changes do you need to make to budget more effectively with each of these commodities?
- What action steps can you take to stay the course?

CHAPTER 3

The Embodied Empath

You are the embodiment of the information you choose to accept and act upon. To change your circumstances, you need to change your thinking and subsequent actions.

—ADLIN SINCLAIR

It's much more fun to dance when you bring your whole body to the party.

—DR. SUE MORTER

All of nature is intended to flourish, prosper, and grow. The bear doesn't worry that it wasn't created as a chimpanzee. A bird doesn't compare one wing to the other and lament over its scrawny little legs. A dandelion does not waste minutes and hours envious and insecure because of the beauty of a rose. The lion never quiets its roar so as not to disturb or intimidate others. All of nature knows how to proclaim its own beauty, purpose, and identity.

But humans, we really screw this up. This despite the fact that "all of nature" includes you. You were created to be as you are—nothing more, nothing less, nothing else, and no one else. What we as Empaths must work toward is what I call *Embodiment*—learning to embrace, utilize, and employ all parts of you, just as you are. Embodiment is the ability to utilize your entire being—mind, body, and spirit in their full capacity—to be present in the world with what's happening around you and what you are experiencing because of it.

Embodiment is a consistent practice of aligning and working in conjunction with your body as an intuitive, entrusted guide composed of magnificent systems, knowledge, and capability. Inside you is a powerful trifecta that provides you with everything you need. That trifecta consists of your mind, body, and spirit. The rapport you have with each of these parts plays a fundamental role in the ways you function in the world. Together, they offer wisdom, guidance, and insight in their own methods and fashion. An embodied union of the three equips you with an all-encompassing awareness and insight that establishes you as the creator and navigator of your life.

There are multiple spheres to consider in the course of this work of Embodiment, and we'll begin with logic and emotion (otherwise stated as the head and the heart). I will introduce a third component later to familiarize you with the beautiful trifecta.

WHO'S COMING ALONG?

Imagine the trip of a lifetime. The plans are set; the timing and route are clear. You're a few minutes late getting out the door, so you dismissively wave at your neighbor when he reminds you for the second time that your tires are low and the windshield has a small crack in it. You politely smile and secretly wish he would mind his own business.

Ten minutes in, you've got to stop for gas and some truck stop snacks to fuel yourself. A few more miles down the road, the check engine light comes on. You ignore it, thinking it will be fine, and besides, who has the time to deal with any of that? You grip the wheel tightly and sit up in your seat to see over that spreading crack in the windshield. You continue to push the gas petal as you turn up the music to drown out that pesky knocking noise you've been hearing more often lately.

Just miles from your destination, you're forced to pull to the side of the frenzied freeway with a shattered windshield and smoke billowing so heavily you can't even see the road. Calling for help would've been a lot easier if you'd purchased that phone charger you'd been meaning to buy.

Can you even imagine? Who would sign up for that trip? Almost instantly, that dream vacation turns into the trip from hell. It's silly really, to believe anyone would approach such an important venture with such little care or concern. And yet, here you are, with an equally important opportunity, a life beckoning you to live, love, and experience each day from a place of preparedness and pleasure.

How intentional and deliberate are you about this thing called life? How well suited are you for the journey? How attentive are you to the "vehicle" you've been granted to navigate through life? How well fueled are you, and are you taking care of things that need your attention and consideration? Are there important factors you're overlooking, minimizing, or neglecting? Have you stopped to consider the toll of these? Do you address things proactively, or do you wait for that whack upside the head that life often delivers when you haven't been listening?

YOUR BODY AS A WHOLE

You've been granted a body as the vehicle for this ultimate journey around the earth. It's an extraordinary thing composed of many working systems and parts, all designed to work in conjunction with each other, and it's important to consider it in its entirety. It's likely there are several parts and systems you pay little attention to, perhaps even neglect, deny, shame, or suppress. As a human equipped with head, heart, brain, breath, feet, belly, and so much more, each of these pieces needs your care and consideration. Just like a vehicle is intended to move you from one place to another safely and effectively, so too is the purpose of your body. The ways you care for, support, and align with your body in its entirety is critical to your overall experience and well-being, especially for Empaths.

Embodiment is the ability to work with your mind, body, and intuition in unison and properly attune to and care for each part. Imagine trying to be in tip-top shape and working out only your arms without acknowledging your legs, cardio, etc. Or cleaning the kitchen but never putting a cloth to any other part of your home, washing your feet but no other part of your body, mowing the backyard but not the front. It's all so absurd, and yet that may be exactly how you're treating your body, focusing on only one part while ignoring or neglecting the others. Embodiment is the use, care, and practice of all your body.

Specific behaviors and practices enable you to function from an empowered, energized place to utilize these parts effectively, establishing a firm foundation for you to function consciously, and be well equipped for daily interactions and basic living.

Draw your attention to your earlobe—your left earlobe, to be exact. Enhance your awareness by touching it, tugging on it, stretching it, noticing any sensation. How does it feel? Obviously, for most people, your left earlobe was there all along, but the intentional noticing drew attention to it and allowed you to use, feel, and move it in different ways. So it is with awareness and Embodiment. It is deliberately calling focus and use to all parts of yourself to be present with your body in full.

Being mindful that every part of you is important and meant to be respected establishes standards and conditions that support optimal health and well-being. Holding high respect for the power and wisdom of your body—with its needs, preferences, and feelings—is a profound way to approach daily life. Consistent, deliberate attention to your mind, body, and spirit are imperative. It allows you to establish yourself as a priority, access information on different levels, live from an empowered stance, and utilize the wisdom and insight the body holds.

What is your opinion of your body? How much do you honor and respect it? Are there parts that you loathe and scorn? Are you able to love and appreciate it the way it deserves, or do you neglect, abuse, and ridicule it? What behaviors or conditions are you allowing? Just like that crack in the windshield, are you ignoring problems until they become much bigger? Are you fueling up on junk, mistreating and misusing your body?

Your thoughts and beliefs set the foundation that determines your perspective, tolerance, decisions, and self-talk. Assessing the health and quality of this inner system allows you to heal and improve specific areas of your life and be fully embodied.

TAMING THE WILD BEAST

Let's return to our analogy of that dreaded trip. This time, imagine that you also have a copilot who's along for the ride, a passenger who judges and criticizes everything you do. The person finds fault, critiques, and berates you. They're extreme and take everything personally. They're demanding, insensitive, and condemning. They drink too much, complain, gossip, and eat all the snacks.

Could you imagine a worse companion? How much would you dread the time spent, their input and feedback? Would you trust or buy into anything they had to say? Every mile would turn to misery.

Something to consider . . . Are *you* that person? Are you the one who abuses and mistreats yourself? The one who scrutinizes and belittles yourself, constantly evaluating what's wrong with you, assessing every little move through a critical eye? Do you ruminate on your weaknesses and missteps while ignoring the essence of who you are? Are you behaving poorly or allowing people or circumstances to exist that are destructive to you? Are your daily habits and patterns of thought unhealthy and destructive? Here's a reality check: Are you someone you would want to companion with you if you had the choice?

We live in a world that emphasizes perfection and unrealistic standards for the body. With the pressures of filters, fillers, facials, fakes, followers, and fans, there is constant demand to be something other than who and what you are. Scrutinizing eyes and incessant self-criticism may be so focused on flaws, that you override and overlook the value and purpose of your body. Perhaps you've succumbed to worldly pressures and expectations and held unrealistic standards, causing you to lose touch with your gifts and purpose.

Familial, societal, religious, and cultural traditions, teachings, roles, and beliefs shape your view and understanding of your body, along with its purpose and value. Further, messages surrounding food, and your worth associated with physical beauty and weight often reinforce messages of body-shaming, condemnation, sinfulness, loathing, punishment, loathing, and self-denial. Confidence, assurance, and esteem are often noted as pride, arrogance, and haughtiness.

Misinformation and generations of misguided beliefs have distorted the significance of the body, causing mass disruption, destruction, disconnect, and disrepair. Most of society, and Empaths in particular, are seeking solace in any way possible, most of these methods equally problematic as the original issue. Solutions that reinforce numbing and suppression lead to tragic issues of addiction, disorders, depression, anxiety, suicide, and violence. We're in a world that's increasingly disconnected from the most prized resource of all—the body.

You may have been taught to ignore, suppress, deny, and disregard your body, its needs, and personal value. You may be at war with your body, having spent years working against it, in constant confusion, berating, and doubt. Perhaps it's been a lifetime of denying, controlling, shaming, and chastising your body, its needs, sensations, and cues. The tool of Embodiment allows you to embrace and appreciate your body and work in alignment and conjunction with it to develop an intimate, trusting relationship as you rely on the wisdom, insight, and gifts it holds.

My friend, the buck stops here. It is in this moment that you become fully aware of and responsible for the neglect and torment you're causing yourself. You take you with you wherever you go, and your thoughts and beliefs are a key factor in determining the quality of your life.

HEAD AND HEART

There are two distinct dimensions to consider in body wisdom: the head (logic and reason) and the heart (emotion and sense). The thoughts you entertain are the fuel of the mind, and feelings you experience are the language of the heart. The head thinks and the heart feels. Actually, the entire body feels, but we'll talk about that more later. You are equipped with the power and magnitude of both sources, yet, people often have fragmented parts within their body tapping into limited parts of their capabilities.

Can you imagine a head without a heart or a heart without a head? They need one another, and you cannot separate the two effectively.

The human body is magnificent, equipped with multisensory parts and systems connected and interwoven to allow you to experience and enjoy life. Though separate and distinct in the way they experience and perceive information, the head and heart influence and inform one another, hold powerful information and insight, and are intended to work in conjunction.

You may have a dominant, instinctual way you perceive the world. Maybe your mind is in charge; you're very logical and strategic, and you need to make sense of what's happening in and around you. On the other hand, you may experience the world heart-first and have more emotional responses to what's going on.

Neither is right or wrong. Head and heart are intended to support and fortify you when applied in conjunction. Utilizing both logic and emotion makes you a powerhouse in your own right. Just like touch and taste are different sensory experiences, or feet and hands are different body parts, the head and heart are equally important and will enhance your experience when used together.

Though they are a source of incredible information, emotions tend to be dismissed, minimized, criticized, and deemed unreliable. We've heard terms such as *dramatic*, *histrionic*, *extreme*, *overly sensitive*, *neurotic*, *prima donna*, and *exaggerated* to describe folks with big emotion. If you are emotionally dominant in how you experience the world, you may have received a lot of critical messages about who you are and how you process the world.

Empaths are often chastised, misunderstood, and made fun of for the ways they feel so deeply and the things they perceive that others don't. Have you learned to suppress or deny your emotions? Do you feel a level of shame, confusion, or inadequacy because of how you're wired and the things you've been told about yourself?

Logic and reason, on the other hand, tend to be more highly valued and esteemed. Yet, they only offer information from one realm. The mind does not cover the entire gamut of someone's experience. Functioning strictly from a place of logic without consideration for emotion limits the perspective and your ability to fully navigate the world and relationships.

The two parts, head and heart, make a far more effective whole. Your embodied use of emotion to sense and inquire, coupled with the mind to investigate and think things through, allows you to fully encompass your experiences and aligns you with critical information from both sources—the heart, with its primal, instinctual, intuitive information, along with the mind that offers intellect, logic, and reasoning. In the pages to come, we will address practices for witnessing both.

Which is the stronger sense for you: head or heart?

On a scale of 1–10, rate the following (1 IS NOT AT ALL; 10 IS COMPLETELY):

I know how to use both heart and head in decision-making and navigating life.

1	2	3	4	5	6	7	8	9	10

Specific things role modeled or taught about logic vs. emotion:
Example: Don't be a crybaby. Use your head.

1.

2.

3.

INTUITION—TAPPING IN

*The intellect has little to do on the road to discovery.
There comes a leap of consciousness, call it intuition or
what you will, and the solution comes to you and you
don't know how or why.*

—ALBERT EINSTEIN

As you embrace the faithful companions of head and heart, I'll introduce you to another player in this game: intuition, also known as a hunch, the gut, or a sixth sense. You've probably experienced that gut sense about someone or something, or an impulse to take an action. There's no rhyme or reason to it, but you do feel it. It may even seem to defy logic or what you think you know. Just as brain and heart have different purposes, so too does your intuition. It is your most powerful guide, far above logic, emotions, old beliefs, internal stories, and social training. It is a knowing that is directly linked to a deeper, wiser side of you.

Intuition can be defined as "the ability to understand something immediately, without the need for conscious reasoning," or "a thing that one knows or considers likely from instinctive feeling rather than conscious reasoning" (Oxford Languages). Intuition is like a friendly, ever-present visitor awaiting permission to align, assist, and speak with you. It will knock at the door, but it needs to be invited in. Intuition uses emotion and sensory cues to communicate to the body to deliver important information. In this way, it becomes the final (and equally important) component of the trifecta that is Embodiment.

Developing and consistently utilizing Embodiment practices allows you to cultivate a relationship in which you rely on the head, heart, and intuition to be your most powerful guides and trusted resources.

MINDFUL OVERLOAD

The body knows what's in your best interest, and it will do its best to communicate with you. It's critical to know the signs and methods it uses to speak to and inform you. A sudden sense of confusion or uncertainty is likely a cautious whisper. Panic or dread that seems to come from nowhere is probably a warning call telling you to take heed. A sense of wonderment and curiosity can be an intuitive nudge to move further, make the call, ask the question, see what's possible. These emotions and sensations are nudges, caution calls, and directives.

Embodiment allows you to distinguish between your body intelligence versus worldly pressures, old stories, others' expectations, and feelings of fear and anxiety. All your answers lie within, and as an Empath, you have intuitive powers to guide, direct, and protect you at every turn. However, there are many obstacles that can distract and confuse you or dilute your intuition.

In just one second, the brain receives almost four hundred billion bits of information. Just *one* second! In the course of twenty-four hours, adults are said to make an average of thirty-five thousand decisions. This is staggering to think about! Every day, you face tens of thousands of decisions, many of them subconscious and habitual. Brain fatigue can easily set in, especially during times of stress or exhaustion. Everyday living can be incredibly taxing.

The good news is the brain does not have to do all the work by itself. When you learn to tap into mind, body, and intuition, you will have all you need to make decisions, carry on conversations, and assess what's right and wrong for you. How often after the fact do you exclaim "*I knew it!*"? That knowing often occurs on all three levels and is a powerful guidance system that will guide and direct you if you allow it to.

Whether you're trying to decide upon a specific course of action, a treatment modality, which exercise is best, a job opportunity, a marriage proposal, or coping mechanisms, the body intuitively knows and will tell you what's in your best interest when you learn to tune in and trust what it's saying. Embodied practices help you filter through and regulate your experiences to manage and direct the energy you're exposed to, allowing you to decipher what's best. Rather than being flooded and overwhelmed by the signs and symptoms or wanting to deny, avoid, numb, or suppress these sensations, embodied practices allow you to embrace and regulate your experiences fully.

Margorie was excited and committed to her new fitness goals, so she scheduled an appointment with a local trainer. She loved the facility and appreciated the time and attention the trainer gave her in the appointment, scheduling a regimen for her, offering a free week, and introducing her to other clients. The location was perfect and class times fit perfectly into Margorie's schedule. There was nothing left to do but sign the contract. Just as she took the pen, she felt a slight nudge of hesitancy and resistance. She excused herself to the restroom and took a moment to tune in. Something didn't feel right.

The mental chatter began. "But everyone is so nice. They've offered you so much of their time and have been so helpful. There you go again, finding every reason not to get healthy." She was conscious of that voice and the pressure to accommodate and appease others.

Margorie walked back to the desk feeling uncertain and uncomfortable. Her mind was racing, her stomach in knots. She knew what she needed to do.

"You folks have been so kind, and I am going to take the contract home to look it over. When I've made a decision, I'll be in touch. Thank you."

"But I don't understand," the trainer said. "Did we do something wrong? It would be nice to get this signed and taken care of today so we can get you started this week. How about I throw in another week free?"

"Again, you are so kind. It's just that I always feel better sitting with my decisions before I sign. I'll be in touch. Thanks again for your time."

Marjorie took the contract and left. In the car, she felt her shoulders relax, her stomach begin to settle, and the tension in her legs ease. "Something wasn't right," she reinforced to herself.

Upon reviewing the contract, the print was very fine, but Marjorie saw the issue immediately. She would be locked in for two years, and should she want to cancel, she would be charged the entire amount up front from the bank account they required to be on file. Like a puzzle piece that finally fits, she saw the dilemma and was confirmed in her intuitive *knowing*.

OFF THE RAILS

Pollution, which I will also refer to as "rubbish," is a very real thing that affects you in ways you're not even aware of. Life is full of rubbish that distracts and confuses the intuition and pollutes the body. As we saw with that trip of a lifetime, there are issues that need to be paid attention to and managed. The more proactive and mindful you are, the more in tune you will be, but the mind and body can easily become contaminated with things that infiltrate and infect. You may be plagued by the tendency to please, opinions of others, toxins, chaos, busyness, disruptions, false beliefs, unhealthy behaviors, and misinformation. Some of these things are obscure, habitual, and subconscious, but they're there, nonetheless. It's easy to overlook, minimize, excuse, and justify these toxins.

Your daily choices impact the quality of your life, and your intuition may be lying dormant under layers of this rubbish. It's important to assess the rubbish that pollutes your mind, body, and spirit. You may not recognize how you've been influenced by each of these. Just like a thick film pasted over your glasses will skew your view and warp your perspective, so will this rubbish distort your view and ability to tune in to your intuition.

WHAT'S THE RUBBISH?

1. **Nourishment:**

Common sense tells you not to put sawdust into a gas tank. A plant won't be around long if planted in a pile of rocks without water. What are you feeding your body? Are you practicing due diligence to care for and maintain it to its fullest capacity? Have you fallen prey to the societal permission of convenience and immediate gratification that promote ease over quality?

We all know that what goes into something will eventually define the health, quality, and longevity of it. What do you allow to go into your mind, body, and spirit? What's the quality of food, drink, substances, and products you're being exposed to? What are you allowing to exist in your life, and have you taken the time to assess the health and quality of how these things impact you? Can you see how the things you eat, drink, listen to, and engage in impact the trifecta of mind, body, and spirit?

Wholesome nourishment is critical to your physical, mental, emo-tional, and spiritual health. Whether you see your body as a temple, a well-oiled machine, or an old, dilapidated piece of junk, how you fuel it matters. The quality and quantity of what you allow will influence the overall health of each of these, and it is solely up to you determine what's in your best interest.

Food, as commonplace and necessary as it is, is also quite complex and multifaceted. Though its purpose is to fuel your body, most people have a very distorted relationship with it. Using food to cope, numb, distract, reward, love, punish, deprive, connect, buffer, or relate can be not only destructive and habitual, but it can also become addictive and deadly. These patterns confuse the basic purpose of nourishment and obscure the innate sense of true hunger and fullness. They disconnect you from your own mind, body, and spirit.

As an Empath, how do you use food? Can you see longstanding patterns and behaviors that impact your body? Do you use food to distract, stuff, deprive, punish, or deny your body? Do you overeat or undereat, use it to cope, or numb yourself?

Let's get real—can we even call it food anymore with the horrifying list of chemicals, additives, and preservatives companies put in the foods we eat? Sugar, dyes, high-fructose corn syrup, caffeine, salt, and artificial sweeteners are highly addictive substances, and most of them are chemicals, not food. The impact of these substances can be very destructive to your mental, physical, and emotional well-being. What type of nourishment are you allowing? How would you rate the quality of food you're eating? Are there habits, patterns, or addictions that need your attention?

Empaths may deal with food sensitivities and react more strongly to chemicals, additives, and other substances. Though most people are impacted by these in some way, Empaths have heightened systems, making them more susceptible. Recognizing not only your approach and relationship with food, but also the influence of various foods, will be a necessary work for your overall health. Small changes can make a big difference.

- What is your relationship with food?
- How did you learn to use food this way?
- What is the quality of food you choose to put in your body?
- What impact is this having on you?
- What are one or two small changes you are ready to make or experiment with?

2. Drink:

Water covers more than 70 percent of Earth's surface, and the human body is said to be about 65 percent water. Most humans know they should drink more water but are challenged to do so. The staggering statistic is that 75 percent of the American population is not only dehydrated but *chronically dehydrated*. This despite drinking water being one of the easiest, most cost-effective, and readily available resources you can achieve without much effort or risk to you.

Maybe you're just thirsty?

- Irritability
- Listlessness
- Lightheaded
- Headache
- Drowsy
- Problems with excretion
- Dizziness
- Dry mouth
- Poor body temperature
- Joint aches and pains
- Weakness
- Cramping

Drink more water . . . period! We all know we should, but few do it. It's one of the simplest ways you can take better care of yourself. Sorry to be the bearer of bad news, but alcohol, sports drinks, and coffee don't count.

It's not uncommon for Empaths to use substances and chemicals to alter their emotional state, using them to somehow shift their state up or down. Do you have to have those five cups of coffee to get through your day? Are you reaching for your afternoon boost to help cope with stress, fatigue, and other difficult states? Are you using alcohol to numb? Does a glass or two, or five, help knock off the stress of the day? Do you need to have a glass in your hand to regulate your social experiences? What does alcohol do for you that you don't know how to do without it?

Toxins of both food and drink will mentally and emotionally clog and disrupt the power of your trifecta and distort the signs and symptoms your body uses to talk to you.

Can you commit to increasing your water consumption daily? What's a realistic goal, and how can you hold yourself accountable?

3. **External Influences:**

Empaths are sensitive to the thoughts, energy, and feelings of others, and it doesn't take much for them to sense and discern other people's needs and preferences. Perhaps you've learned to prioritize other voices and opinions over your own. Maybe your thoughtfulness and consideration has gone too far and you've suppressed, overridden, minimized, or discredited your own perspective and perception.

Having any type of strong influencer in your life, such as an overbearing parent, an obnoxious sibling, a taunting neighbor, a dismissive teacher, or a boisterous boss can weigh heavily and shape how you feel about yourself, the ways you learn to show up in the world, or how you assert your voice. As an Empath, maybe you've formed yourself into what you believe others want, adapting and acclimating to what's expected of you or approved of by others. You may consider someone else more of an expert over your life than you are. You may not know how to process their reactions, opinions, or energy, so you've tuned your internal radar outward to sense and detect what's right for others, more so than for yourself.

Your perception, the things you do and don't do, your opinions and preferences, outlook, behavior, mood, choices, attitude, and definition of "normal" may all be determined through the lens of others, with little regard to what you think or prefer. Consider how you weigh others' feelings and preferences in your daily life to see if there are some changes you need to make. Run your beliefs through a clear lens. Take the time to think about what you're thinking about and what you've subscribed to as truth. It's important awareness.

The influences that impact the way you think and what you believe extend beyond the people you know. Years ago, advertising was limited to things such as mailers, radio, billboards, TV, etc. Reach was reduced to local communities and nearby listening and viewing areas. In today's world, we are assaulted with advertisements at every turn, and in multiple capacities. It has been estimated that the average person sees nearly ten thousand ads each day. You can't hide from the powerful punch of these messages, and the ways they influence and shape your outlook and perspective. The impact they have, even subconsciously, is profound. What are you allowing to filter in?

When you add the social, cultural, peer, and religious persuasion that Empaths feel, it is safe to say your Sense of Self and ability to differentiate or gain autonomy is greatly impacted. Social media, news, music, religion, and culture weigh heavily on an Empath's sense of basic concepts, such as right, wrong, ideal, healthy, beautiful, thin, happy, etc. As an Empath, you must strongly consider what you're giving attention to and what you've taken on as *truth*.

Intuition is often a nudge or whisper that's easily silenced or drowned out by the persuasive energy of these influences. If you've learned to prioritize opinions other than your own, or have fallen prey to pressure, norms, standards, expectations, fear, limitations, and rules, it may take some time to learn to trust and honor the insight and wisdom of that powerful trifecta of mind, body, and spirit. Experiencing the world with the use of your entire body while honoring and respecting your insight, senses, and intuitive knowing will guide you through decisions and circumstances. Aligning with those innate nudges and gut feelings will strengthen that intrinsic voice.

What you pay attention to and give priority to matters. Like an undeveloped muscle that needs to be stretched and worked out, so too is your intuition. If it's become silenced or atrophied, your intuition will strengthen with consistent practice and effort. An embodied practice and a commitment to this work allows you to build into the intuitive skillset. Intuition will benefit from your unconditional reliance, practice, and exercise to strengthen and intensify its power.

A GPS (Global Positioning System) will take you almost anywhere you need to go if you turn it on and listen to its guidance. You are equipped with your own internal GPS (Gut, Perception, and Senses), that's intended to be your voice of reason and direction, far outweighing the input and opinions of others. Enlightenment allows you to enhance your relationship with it and use it to navigate your course in life. This is your most powerful guidance system that leads and directs you where you need to go, but only when you tune in to it and trust where it's taking you.

Whether you recognize it or not, your GPS speaks to you. It may be a nudge, a sense of *knowing*, dread, anxiety, angst, or a tiny whisper.

Are you familiar with it? When you feel the pressure of those external influences, do you know how to tune inward and inquire from your own navigational system? Are you able to appreciate its purpose and value? Are you willing to explore and enhance your GPS and your relationship with it?

4. Religion

You are a spiritual being having a physical, mental, emotional, and divine experience here on Earth. Your religious experience is highly influential in defining your sense of good and bad, right and wrong, dos and don'ts, acceptable and unacceptable. The spiritual realm is filled with messages, stories, themes, and belief systems that are fundamental in shaping your understanding of yourself, a higher power, and the "rules" of the world.

As an Empath who senses and feels on a different level, you probably have some connection with or attunement toward something other-worldly. You may not know what it is or be able to define it, but there is likely some type of spiritual rousing inside of you.

Even as a young child, Aubrey remembers crying in church because she felt the energy of the people and music. The adults were confused by her tears, and she was chastised, often told to "knock it off" and that she was being silly and overreacting. She was too young and too overwhelmed to name what she felt or why; she just knew that the flooding emotion in the church didn't feel like it was hers. It felt like it was happening *to* her, and she had no idea how to contain it. She still remembers how that punishing feeling left her with a bad sense about herself and religion.

No matter your understanding or experience with religion, you've probably been exposed to some of the traditional messages, teachings, lessons, stories, players, etc. Religion can be the source of much love, connection, inspiration, and hope. Many of the stories and themes are beautiful, inspiring, and compassionate. On the other hand, there is significant controversy, conflict, argument, and even wars stemming from religious debates. The premise is often fear-based, demonized, sacrificial, martyred, persecuting, and punishing. Difference is not encouraged or accepted, and the body is thought to be sinful and not to be trusted.

Religion may teach specific standards, expectations, and rules that leave you questioning your gifts, sensory experiences, and level of emotion to determine what is and what's not acceptable. Your gifts and insights may be deemed sacrilegious and sinful without proper understanding. Being wired as deeply as you are may feel confusing, shameful, or sinful, so you've learned to deny, shame, or suppress parts of yourself.

Being taught to deny your body, that you are a sinner, to quash your needs or gifts, to succumb to blind submission, to make martyred attempts to put others before yourself, or to honor absolute authority impacts your beliefs, behaviors, thought process, perspective, Sense of Self, and coping mechanisms. There is a time and place for sacrifice, service, submission, and suppression, but without context or balance, these can create extremes, division, lack of safety and well-being, along with rigid fundamentalism—especially for an Empath. It is critical to assess what you believe and the impact of these beliefs to determine if they align with your deeper truth and knowing.

You have every right to decide what to believe, what serves you best, what kind of person you want to be, what morals and values you hold, what kind of relationships you want to have with the God of your understanding, and what your practice/worship looks like. It's most important to understand old messages and beliefs you've received from family, culture, and past experiences to determine what you want to subscribe to.

I was taught the following about God:

1.

2.

3.

The God of my understanding is:

1.

2.

3.

On a scale of 1–10, rate the following (1 IS NOT AT ALL; 10 IS COMPLETELY):

These beliefs & practices serve me well:

1	2	3	4	5	6	7	8	9	10

5. Poor Sense of Self:

If anyone said life was easy, I don't think they were telling the truth. There are trials and tribulations we face, and life will either be enjoyed or endured during different seasons. Early childhood experiences, family messages, peers, social status, learning struggles, making the team, not making the team, getting your heart broken—all these things influence and shape what you believe about yourself.

Your SOS (Sense of Self) is your ability to know who you are, your own opinions, strengths, limitations, and capabilities. It can be defined through your beliefs, confidence, esteem, strengths, capabilities, talents, and value you hold about who and what you are. It also includes your ability to manage, soothe, and regulate your emotions and experiences.

Everything along the way influences and shapes your SOS. It is defined by what did happen as much as what didn't happen. Even with as important as it is, rarely do people stop to assess or evaluate their SOS.

I would describe myself in the following ways:

1.

2.

3.

My strengths include:

1.

2.

3.

4.

5.

On a scale of 1–10, rate the following (1 IS NOT AT ALL; 10 IS COMPLETELY):

I have a solid Sense of Self & know the qualities I possess.

| 1 | 2 | 3 | 4 | 5 | 6 | 7 | 8 | 9 | 10 |

I'm aware of my faults & can keep them in perspective of myself as a whole.

| 1 | 2 | 3 | 4 | 5 | 6 | 7 | 8 | 9 | 10 |

I have the skills and tools I need to cope & feel good about myself.

| 1 | 2 | 3 | 4 | 5 | 6 | 7 | 8 | 9 | 10 |

You can begin to see the weight of these influences and the ways they shaped your identity and functioning. Most, though likely intended for good, have influenced key dynamics of how you feel and relate that deserve your reflection and assessment. Moving forward, it's up to you to decide what's in your best interest and what you want to redefine for your personal growth and well-being.

Life as an Empath can be extra challenging and confusing when you don't understand what you're experiencing. Imagine a child growing up with learning differences and developing a core belief that he or she is stupid and incapable, until that one teacher sees the issue and introduces them to their specific learning style. The whole world opens up because someone is finally teaching in a way a child can understand. Or imagine a person in a foreign country not knowing anyone or even how to utter a single word of the native tongue, when suddenly they hear a voice speaking their language. The joy and elation would be remarkable.

Empaths often feel as though something is wrong with them, that they speak another language, or don't fit a typical mold. Taking the time to really know and understand yourself while identifying your strengths and capabilities—as well as to care for and cultivate tools, coping mechanisms, self-care practices, resources, and a community that embraces and supports you—will be necessary to eliminate and quiet the impact of the rubbish affecting you.

Strengthening and building your Sense of Self will empower you to develop your skills and feel confident about who you are and how to use your gifts. Knowing how to recognize and eliminate the rubbish, foster healthy habits for rest and refueling, and entertain only productive beliefs, connection, and routines will generate trust in your body, mind, and intuition. You will start to see each of these as valuable sources of information, guidance, and direction. As you inquire and get curious about what the mind, body, and spirit are communicating through your senses, you will honor and respect the wise counsel they offer.

Honor what one might call the sacred trinity of mind, body, and spirit and the importance each one carries. Work in alignment and conjunction with the body, not against it. Your body knows. Listen to and cooperate with what it is communicating. Denying, suppressing, or shaming your physical cues is a personal betrayal that ultimately creates more damage and consequence.

On a scale of 1–10, rate the following (1 IS NOT AT ALL; 10 IS COMPLETELY):

I take good care of myself.

| 1 | 2 | 3 | 4 | 5 | 6 | 7 | 8 | 9 | 10 |

I have daily habits & routines that serve me well.

| 1 | 2 | 3 | 4 | 5 | 6 | 7 | 8 | 9 | 10 |

Practices that no longer serve me:

1.

2.

3.

As an Empath, practices & routines that best support me include the following:

1.

2.

3.

BODY WISDOM

Have you ever felt unheard, not understood, or desperate to convey your message? I often wonder if that's not how the body feels most of the time. Your body always knows what it needs and has developed specific methods to speak to and inform you. Are you hearing what your body wants and needs?

As your own wisest counsel, you have all the answers. Now it's time to listen. You already have everything you need for this journey. The mind, body, and spirit are informational systems that convey details and insight intended to guide and direct you.

The body communicates and leaves evidence of its needs. A good night's sleep, a joyful spirit, healthy elimination, or the ability to walk, run, smile, or skip are indicators typically informing you that all systems are a go and things are moving along well. Equally important to consider are cues such as ache, pain, hunger, constipation, exhaustion, angst, sleep disturbance, or a gnawing gut sense. The body *knows*, and wants your attention and respect to honor, care for, and safeguard it.

A parent of a toddler works to decipher and interpret the gibberish and gestures of their young child to develop communication and connection. So too can you decode and clarify the insight and wisdom of your body. Inquire and listen to the messages and cues.

As an Empath who is at risk of absorbing the emotion, energy, and experience of others as well as your own, you may be plagued by energy and emotion that become stuck or clogged within your system. Developing a respectful relationship with your body is imperative, along with consistent practices of regulating and expelling emotion and energy, to enable you to discern the somatic information you're experiencing.

An Embodiment practice allows you to inquire and recognize your specific signs and symptoms to distinguish your experience from that of someone else. A pain in your head or a gnawing sense in your belly may be trying to communicate a basic need for care and rest, or it may be an intuitive warning to watch out, pay attention, or take action. A sense of dread and panic may mean that you need to cancel some plans, or it may be a feeling you are getting from another person. Signs and symptoms of stress, strain, discomfort, and unease are ways your body is notifying you of something that needs your attention. Your body is speaking to you all the time; are you listening to what it's trying to say?

TUNING IN TO THE BODY

The body is gifted with multiple sensory capabilities—sight, sound, taste, touch, etc. It's likely that these are so commonplace, you don't give them much consideration. Though you may not be conscious of or in tune with your senses, they are valuable sources of information and will enhance your experiences in life. It's like seeing all the colors of the rainbow rather than just black and white. Sensory awakening and attention will enhance your experience if you're in tune with it.

During your next meal, sit down and savor what's in front of you. Look at the food, the colors, and textures, what it's served on, the utensils you're using and the sleek feel of them. Take one small portion and smell it. Touch your tongue to it and feel the temperature. Allow yourself to taste the food. Relish each bite and take your time. Whole new experience, isn't it?

Next up, shower time! As you're preparing to clean your body, take a moment to look at yourself. Use your eyes to take in your body. Enough already with the scrutinizing and criticism. We're not doing that here! Take in the image you see before you with your eyes. Use your fingertips to feel the texture of your skin. Listen to the sound of the water. Allow your hands to touch it and experience the temperature of the cold droplets as the water begins to warm. As you enter, feel water against your skin as you stand there. Allow the water to drench your body, your face, your head.

If you're so courageous, turn the water to cold and embrace the frigid nature of those drops, then restore the heat to experience the difference and impact to your mind and body. Smell the soap and feel the lather of it in your hands. Use your imagination to visualize your stress and worries washing down the drain as you stand refreshed and renewed. Do all this and you may have a hard time getting out of the shower!

When was the last time you felt the grass under your feet as you stood barefoot on the earth? Use your eyes to take in the majesty of a tree. Feel it, touch it, smell it, and go ahead . . . hug it. We'll wait for you! There's power and beauty in nature, and Empaths are deeply affected by the splendor of it. Spend as much time in nature as you can. Find every reason to get outside, take in the fresh air, and feel the earth underneath your feet. This is a very grounding, centering practice.

The pace of the world tends to be a fast one. It's likely that you rush through your day, missing opportunities to be present in your body and use your senses to witness, enjoy, and experience your surroundings. You can decide at any point to integrate your whole body and each of your senses into your daily routine to enhance and tantalize your experiences. It's magical when you do this, as it allows you to be truly present in life.

Sensory cues are the ways the body takes in and experiences information to communicate with you and assess circumstances. Below is a list of different bodily experiences to take into consideration.

SENSORY CUES

Sight	Sound	Smell	Gut
Taste	Texture	Touch	Temperature
Balance	Tone	Pain / Discomfort	Breathing

Is there a sudden pain in your stomach every time you encounter a specific person or consider going someplace? Do you feel a cold chill or a wave of heat when you walk into a room? Do you experience a change in your breathing when an opportunity presents itself? Are you knocked off-kilter with a sense of dread and dizziness at the invitation to another family event?

These experiences can easily be dismissed or overlooked. It's critical not to do that. Learn to cultivate a relationship with your senses and inquire about peculiar intuitive alerts. Feelings or sensations that seemingly come out of nowhere are likely important messengers. Seek information and insight from them to guide and inform you in everyday tasks such as making decisions, gaining clarity, moving energy, and regulating emotions. Enlist their assistance and wisdom and know you can rely on this trusted source.

BODILY FUNCTIONS: WHAT IS GOING ON?

Water needs to move and flow freely. We've all heard about or witnessed the devastating consequences of when water gets obstructed. One way or another, it will find a way through. It will move over or under things; it will maneuver around all types and sizes of obstacles, and if it can't, pressure will build, things will burst, and disaster will ensue.

Similarly, energy is also intended to move and flow. Your body is designed to use, process, and rid itself of energy as needed. As you learn to experiment with energy and develop your skills and further your Embodiment practices, you'll notice different things beginning to stir and trying to flow out of or through you. Your body, in an effort to clear energy, will naturally do some of the work with various somatic symptoms—yawning, throat clearing, sneezing, bowel movements, thirst, fatigue, etc. It will purge and cleanse, perhaps trying to move old, blocked energy. It may also be trying to filter current experiences in new ways as you're learning to use your body and senses differently.

Tracy is an energy healer I worked with for years. She would commonly yawn throughout our sessions. Finally, I asked, "Are you not getting enough sleep at night? You yawn a lot." She laughed and explained that yawning was the way she moved energy out of her body. She picked up on this fact while working on the energy of other people. She needed to move it out of her body so as not to absorb it from her clients. And here I thought she just needed a nap!

A client named Mary reported that she often had loose bowels and gas when she started her Embodiment work. She was practicing this work and was increasingly aware of the power of her thoughts, words, and behaviors when she caught herself one day commenting about "a bunch of shit she needed to let go of," and her body took her literally.

Don noticed how often he felt the need to clear his throat. Most of his personal work was focused on finding his voice, tuning in to and honoring his intuition, and speaking directly to others rather than his old habits of denying and suppressing his needs. The need to clear his throat cued him in to the reality that he had words that needed to be spoken, rather than stuffed. Whenever he felt the need to clear, he instead shifted his focus internally to determine what he needed to verbalize.

Just like water, your body will find ways to process energy. You may recognize a few of these somatic symptoms in which the body is trying to move and regulate old and new energy. The body is fascinating, and it wants to work in conjunction with your mind and spirit as you do this work. The goal of Embodiment—using *all* your body to process, regulate, move, and soothe emotion and energy.

BODY SPEAKS

Tingling	Bowels	Thirst	Hunger	Goosebumps
Gut Sense	Nausea	Sweat	Burping	Yikes / Uh-Oh
Congestion	Pain	Sleep	Yawning	Exhaustion / Fatigue

Energy moves through my body in the following ways:

1.

2.

3.

Bodily or somatic cues I experience include the following:

1.

2.

3.

Practices I can use to listen to and honor my body include the following:

1.

2.

3.

MOVE IT!

Heightened senses, deep emotions, dysregulation, and absorption of energy can create a wide range of issues. Embodiment is the ability to recognize, use, and move energy effectively, through breath and body, to process and regulate yourself to lessen overwhelm, overstimulation, and somatic symptoms. If emotion and energy cannot move as fluidly and flowing inside your body just as water is intended to move within its various bodies, they will get stuck, clogged, or blocked in specific areas or systems within you, creating physical and emotional complications.

Embodiment is the practice of honoring what you're experiencing while using the spaciousness of your entire body to experience, embrace, purge, and move energy. Knowing how to do so will empower you to navigate life more effectively and prevent complications.

It's likely that you have a dominant section of or system in your body where energy collects and gets obstructed or blocked. Perhaps you've suffered from headaches, tension and tightness in your chest or shoulders, or digestive issues. Embodiment practices enable a conscious awareness of these symptoms and the information they're trying to convey, using the body to bring energy into and through yourself without allowing it to clog or block anywhere within.

Life is hard, energy gets clogged, and Empaths absorb. These factors need to be dealt with and processed effectively to prevent larger, more serious issues. The ways you experience and cope with emotion, energy, and environment will significantly influence your health and well-being.

Let's compare various coping mechanisms.

CAUTIOUS COPING MECHANISMS

Numbing	Substances	Deprivation	Avoidance
Food	Exercise	Denying	Social Media
Excess	Control	Busyness	Distraction
Stuffing	Suppressing	Rigidity	Codependency
Shopping	Workaholism	Overinvolvement	

Geographical Cures—*moving, quitting a job, breaking up, and moving on to the next thing*

When life hits the fan and things get hard, what do you do? What's your go-to way of handling hurt feelings, hard decisions, tough conversations, and scary life choices? Any of the strategies listed above, when used regularly, fail to move or regulate energy and will perpetuate the stress and strain of the situation. Though some of them may provide temporary relief or distraction, they have their own way of making bad situations worse. Make note of any of these habits to be conscious and aware of them. Catching them early will offer a greater chance of making different choices.

You can run from energy and emotion, but you can't hide. It *will* catch up with you, one way or another. Using these coping strategies to deny, suppress, or escape your personal experience or feelings will simply delay, and even worsen them. When coupled with the rubbish you're saturated with, you can see how easily people become contaminated and clogged.

Embodiment practices empower you to use your body as a source of information and as a competent resource for handling emotion and energy. Honoring your physical and emotional symptoms and utilizing healthy coping will allow you to regulate your experience and manage stressors. Embodiment practices allow you to experience and enjoy life because you know you're capable and knowledgeable to deal with it.

The following are Embodiment practices to develop your coping abilities and empathic skills.

FOUNDATION FOR EMBODIMENT BASICS

1. **Awareness**—Tune in and pay attention to what you're experiencing and what's going on around you. What's happening in your body? What are you seeing, feeling, sensing? Stay alert to your thoughts and sensations inside and outside of you.

2. **Noticing Breath**—As you take a breath, witness your experience without judgment or attempts to alter it. Simply take in your experience and notice how you feel and where your breath goes. This is awareness in conjunction with breath.

3. **GPS (Gut, Perception, and Senses)**—Develop a relationship with the gut and use it as valid, useful information. Learn to tune in and trust what your GPS is telling you. Something might feel uncomfortable or uncertain and is telling you to heed the warning. Like that voice that resoundingly informs you to "turn left in 550 feet," recognize the intuitive nudges and direction of your GPS. Be conscious of and in tune with your body and senses.

4. **Emotional Center**—This is the area of your body where you experience emotion and sensory cues the most. When something happens, where do you feel it? Which part of your body takes on or absorbs specific emotion? For many people, it is the gut, the heart, or right between the eyes. If you don't know, use awareness and Noticing Breath to learn. Pay attention to what you feel and where you're feeling it. Practice self-compassion as you learn to observe and sit with an emotion, rather than judging, ridiculing, or trying to change it. Breathe and send energy and light to and through those parts of the body so that emotion doesn't get stuck. Identify where you experience things in your body and how your body is processing it. Is there an ache in your shoulders, a gnawing sense in your gut, or a cold chill that runs down your spine? This is likely your intuition speaking to or nudging you, or it may be energy that is trying to move through your body. Listen to what it needs and is communicating.

5. **Felt Sense**—This is another connection of your body, senses, feelings, intuition, and perceptions. It is the keen awareness of the cues and indicators you're experiencing. Just like you wouldn't ignore serious physical pain, nor should you ignore emotional pain, discomfort, gnawing thoughts, or intuitive warnings. These are signals that something needs your attention, and the Felt Sense is your awareness of them.

6. **Body Scan**—Head to toe, this is a tool used to recognize and feel into your body. Investigate it in full to see where emotion and energy lie. Is there color, texture, a smell, or a temperature to what you're feeling? Can you feel the blood-red, jagged edges of

that conflict you're having? Can you feel the melting cool liquid of ease and relaxation as you slip into bed? If you imagined your emotion or energy having a sound, what would it be? The loud beating of a big bass drum? The roar of a fierce lioness protecting her young, or the soft purr of a tender new kitten? What is the message trying to come through? What does your body need? What is calling for your attention or effort?

7. **Sensory Check-In**—Tune in to each of the senses we've discussed as you utilize these Embodiment practices. It's like going to the gym and having a whole-body workout in which each muscle group is practiced and strengthened.

   - When you walk into a room, what do you see? What do your eyes focus on? What is the temperature of the room and the smells that are there? What are the colors you're drawn to and the overall feel of the room? How are you affected by these?

   - When you meet someone, what is the feel of the conversation and the gut sense you have? What's the volume, tone, and energy you pick up? What's pleasurable about the experience and what's not? Is there physical touch, or do you want there to be? Can you use your voice to communicate?

   - When you've had a stressful day and are reaching for something to eat or drink, what are you craving and why? Have you taken the time to assess what you're hungry for? Is it really food, is it relief, or is it connection? If it is true hunger, have you taken the time to properly prepare, present, or heat the food you want? How does it taste, and is the texture what you're looking for? Why is that texture important (the crunch of a hard chip or carrot to release some of the tension, the warmth and soothing feel of soup as it slips down your throat)? Are you sitting down and eating from a plate and tending to the food and the hunger, rather than stuffing, numbing, and distracting?

- When you lie down in bed to rest your mind and body, what is the feel, texture, and temperature of the sheets, the blankets, and the pillowcase? What is the temperature of the room? What images pop into your mind? What are the sounds you're noticing, and how do they influence your rest? What is the last thing you see as you close your eyes to drift off to sleep?

Moment by moment, your senses are working like mini detectors gauging bits of information in multiple capacities. Are you paying attention? Your senses will reveal your feelings and needs. Incorporating those insights into your experiences is like watching something on a two-dimensional screen and then suddenly being introduced to the 3D experience. It opens an entirely different world and allows for an experiential practice with your own body.

Andrew came to my office after seeing his doctor and several specialists due to what he described as tightness and fluttering in his chest. Having been granted a clean bill of health, he continued to experience these distressing symptoms and sought my help. He agreed to experiment with the tools of awareness, Felt Sense, and the Body Scan to familiarize himself with specific things he was experiencing.

He quickly realized that emotion came sharply through his chest with a sense of stabbing and nervousness. Rather than panicking and resisting the emotion, he relaxed into it as much as he could to explore what the sensations may be trying to communicate. He allowed the feeling to come rather than resisting or panicking. The Body Scan and Noticing Breath allowed him to get curious about what he was sensing rather than resorting to the use of his old patterns.

Once he got the hang of it and really began to trust his body, he got creative with the sensations. He knew the red-hot flaming lava he felt was attached to a need to speak up and assert himself rather than stuffing or burying his voice. He was able to identify the fiery anger that was attached to deep fear of embarrassment, rejection, or being shut down. He incorporated all those emotions into his workouts to channel them through his sweat and intense burn. He visualized and used intense breath to release his fears. Learning to experience his emotion allowed his GPS to tune him into some decisions and conversations he needed to have to alleviate conflict and job stressors.

Mariana was altogether different. She knew she didn't have any health problems. As a matter of fact, she kept herself in tip-top shape because that's what was expected of her. She did what others wanted her to do and believed she needed to keep up with their pressures and demands. Mariana spent most of her life prioritizing the opinions of others and listening to their voices. She wanted them to be different, more considerate, and aware, and she believed she wouldn't have all this stress and conflict if they would lay off and actually appreciate her.

For Mariana, the Embodiment work centered around awareness and tuning her into her own body. Her externally focused radar took some time to turn inward as she learned to hear and feel what her body was trying to communicate. Eliminating patterns of blame and expectations that others would eventually change allowed her to recognize the tension in her shoulders and jaw, along with the bouts of panic and dread. Embracing her emotional cues allowed her to face the hard reality that if things were going to change, she was going to have to do something different, not wait on others' praise and appreciation. She began to see these as cues and indicators that she was over-tolerating and over-functioning, and her body had been trying to tell her that all along. She was finally able to honor and respect those early warning signs about people or behaviors, so she didn't have the weight of resentment and people-pleasing on her shoulders.

INTUITIVE NUDGE

Your emotion and instinct will nudge and whisper to you, sometimes in ways that don't make sense. They may coax you in a direction that seems confusing, uncertain, or contrary to your plan. You may resist it, think you're crazy, feel confused, or mistake it for a health problem. You may think other people are the problem and are causing unnecessary stress. But people and circumstances are simply opportunities for you to seek wisdom and insight from within. People won't change because you want them to, and circumstances won't alter because you think they're problematic. The opportunity for change lies within you, and your body is offering you consistent information about what to do and when. It's worth considering that your mind, body, and gut are providing cues they want you to listen to even when the course of action calls you to face those fears and worries.

Embodiment is the union of mind, body, and intuition, a dynamic trifecta that develops and strengthens you. Experimenting with these practices to build familiarity and comfort is like spending quality time with a new lover. It is meant to be filled with wonderment, curiosity, and exploration. You're becoming not only educated but also equipped, so familiarize yourself with these practices to establish a firm personal foundation as you move further into this work.

The following is a simple assessment to increase your awareness as you practice your tools and clean up the rubbish. This is important information that will cue you into areas of strength and struggle. Take the time to assess and reflect on the conditions of your life to gain clarity about what you've been allowing and ways you can begin focusing on your own life to create health, well-being, and optimal conditions for empowerment.

AWARENESS ASSESSMENT

On a scale of 1–10, rate the following (1 IS NOT AT ALL; 10 IS COMPLETELY):

My relationship with my body is healthy.

1   2   3   4   5   6   7   8   9   10

I take care of my body and hygiene.

1   2   3   4   5   6   7   8   9   10

I choose quality foods that are healthy for me.

1   2   3   4   5   6   7   8   9   10

I eat too much.

1   2   3   4   5   6   7   8   9   10

I typically use food to do the following:

1.
2.
3.

I don't nourish my body well. I find myself eating too little.

1   2   3   4   5   6   7   8   9   10

I drink enough to support my body.

1   2   3   4   5   6   7   8   9   10

I pay attention to the quality of substances I put in my body. I'm mindful of chemicals, medications, cigarettes/vape, sugar, alcohol, etc.

1   2   3   4   5   6   7   8   9   10

I find myself using social media to numb, distract, or busy myself.

1   2   3   4   5   6   7   8   9   10

I find myself using social media for the following reasons:

1.

2.

3.

The quality of media I follow serves me well (social media, news, podcasts, email subscriptions, feeds, etc.).

1   2   3   4   5   6   7   8   9   10

The quantity of media I consume serves me well.

1   2   3   4   5   6   7   8   9   10

I get consistent exposure to nature, sunshine, and fresh air.

1   2   3   4   5   6   7   8   9   10

I get the quality sleep I need.

1   2   3   4   5   6   7   8   9   10

I get the amount of sleep I need on a regular basis.

1   2   3   4   5   6   7   8   9   10

I allow myself to rest when I need to but don't isolate or lie around needlessly.

1 2 3 4 5 6 7 8 9 10

I allow myself to have quality resting time (scrolling, bingeing versus reading, being artistic).

1 2 3 4 5 6 7 8 9 10

I have quality community I enjoy and can rely on.

1 2 3 4 5 6 7 8 9 10

I focus on quality relationships rather than busyness and activity.

1 2 3 4 5 6 7 8 9 10

When I seek the company of others, it's usually because (connection, celebration versus obligation, loneliness):

1.

2.

3.

My thoughts are healthy, positive, and self-affirming.

1 2 3 4 5 6 7 8 9 10

I overthink and ruminate about things.

1 2 3 4 5 6 7 8 9 10

I meditate regularly.

1 2 3 4 5 6 7 8 9 10

I have a prayer, worship, or reflection practice that connects me to a God of my understanding.

1   2   3   4   5   6   7   8   9   10

My relationship with my intuition is strong.

1   2   3   4   5   6   7   8   9   10

I recognize my intuition in the following ways:

1.

2.

3.

I will strengthen my intuition in the following ways:

1.

2.

3.

I recognize my Emotional Center as the following:

My body cues of stress or overwhelm include the following:

1.

2.

3.

Energy and emotion impact me in the following ways:

1.

2.

3.

I've coped with energy and emotion in the following ways:

1.

2.

3.

Things that make me feel good:

1.

2.

3.

I'm at my best when:

1.

2.

3.

I will express energy and emotion in the following ways:

1.

2.

3.

PERSONAL LEARNING:

CHAPTER 4

Energy

*Choose a different frequency. Negativity vibrates at a
different frequency. Elevate and create positivity and the
negatives will be out of range for you.*

—LEAURA ALDERSON

*Everything is energy. Your thought begins it. Your
emotion amplifies it, and your action increases its
momentum.*

—UNKNOWN

Have you ever walked into a room and immediately felt uncomfortable without knowing why? Are there times when you're suddenly exhausted after talking to someone for just a few moments? Have you ever met a person and instantly not liked them for no evident reason, secretly wondering if you're just a terribly judgy person? Have you excitedly accepted an invitation and then felt the overwhelming need to cancel the day of because you couldn't bear the thought of socializing, even though you love the people you were going to hang out with?

Situations like these can be confusing and frustrating to deal with. Reactions like these seem to come from nowhere and may be difficult to understand, yet they're real and strong. They're based on a sense or vibe you get from someone or something that can't be explained with facts, logic, or reason, and no matter how hard you try, you can't deny, suppress, or shake them off. As challenging as this may be, what you're experiencing is a real, credible source of information. What you're sensing and picking up on is what I call the *force field of energy.*

It's important to know that everything is energy—yes . . . everything! It's all that exists. The invisible field in which it operates has different wavelengths and varying frequencies that emit vibes, some of which impact you with positive feelings, and some of which impact you with negative feelings. Energy can neither be created nor destroyed, but it can be changed, regulated, moved, and altered with different tools and practices.

You are an energetic being, and so these energy fields influence you in multiple (and differing) ways. As an Empath, they can impact and influence you more deeply than most. After all, you possess intuitive senses that allow you to detect energy. You may absorb energy from people, places, and things without even realizing it or fully understanding what it is. Thoughts, moods, and emotions can suddenly become activated and altered as you encounter these different frequencies. Specific body parts or systems such as digestion, sleep, or muscle tension can be affected by the energy you encounter. Emotions, sensations, and gut senses are cues and indicators of the energy you're experiencing.

Awareness empowers you to be awake, alert, and alive at your own wheel. It's an essential tool that allows you to identify energy and utilize specific practices and coping strategies to regulate, manage, and control the flow and frequency of what you're experiencing. Awareness allows you to pay attention and recognize the impact of energy so you can decide how to process it effectively. It is vital to acknowledge what you're feeling, how you've become activated by someone or something, and how your body is handling the frequency and flow of energy.

Energy is a critical component in every aspect of life. It can be elevated, regulated, and shifted with the slightest bit of attention and intentionality once you develop necessary practices. Feel the stress and tension of the day? Move breath into and out of your body to move the strain. Furious about the results that just came in? Give the air five or six fierce jabs to move the anger out of your body or imagine it as hot lava traveling down out of your feet back into the ground. You can become a master at playing with energy and use it to manage your interactions with others, improve your mood and experience, keep energy and emotion from clogging or contaminating, and make decisions about what's in your best interest. These life-force energies that lie beneath logic and social, religious, and familial conditioning allow you to access powerful insight and information that can alter your course at any turn.

VIBE CHECK

VIBE—*"a person's emotional state or the atmosphere of a place as communicated to and felt by others"*
—OXFORD LANGUAGES

VIBE—*"a mood or an atmosphere produced by a particular person, thing, or place"*

—OXFORD LEARNER'S DICTIONARY

I extended my hand to Mary the first time we met. Her flimsy grip and halfhearted handshake matched her averted eye contact as she entered my office. After she sat down, she explained that she'd sought my services because of her lack of confidence and poor assertion, along with difficulty making friends and her sense of rejection in the dating world. During our session, she spoke just above a whisper and apologized for most of what she said.

Belinda was another story. She shook my hand so firmly, it took a few minutes for the feeling to come back to my fingers. Her voice was so loud, I worried that the neighboring suites might think an argument was unfolding in my office. Her energy was hard, prickly almost. One of her chief complaints was that people were put off by her—so much so, she was written up at work for intimidating others. She simply couldn't understand why this was happening.

Have you ever thought about the energy you carry or the vibe you give off? Have you considered how you show up in the world? These are important points to ponder because they influence the way you interact, how people respond to you, the message you send, and the people you attract. Your thoughts, habits, and moods create an air about you even when you can't sense or detect it. People feel it from you and will react consciously and subconsciously to the sense they get as a result. I am not suggesting you chameleon yourself to accommodate others. I'm simply encouraging you to be aware of how you use and experience energy when socializing or engaging.

You're not born with beliefs that you're unworthy, too much, or not enough. Babies don't concern themselves with what others' think of them or engage in behaviors that result in playing small, feeling insecure, or being riddled with self-doubt. These are false beliefs and patterns of relating that are learned and become ingrained over time. Fortunately, they can also be deconstructed and improved with a firm decision and continued practice.

Your vibe is a result of life experiences and trained responses you've learned along the way, so the act of changing it typically boils down to awareness, intentionality, and choice. You can always choose differently. You will serve others and yourself so much more effectively when you are clearly aligned with who you really are.

Like mindful eating, intentional spending, or any other deliberate habit you've practiced before, you can choose a healthier mindset, improved thoughts and beliefs, along with aligned actions that improve your vibe. It's a daily decision about the way you engage in the world and the energy you bring to the table. Do you love begin around positive people? Practice begin more positive, praising and complimenting others, and notice specific things to be grateful for to improve your vibe. This allows your healthiest, most authentic self to shine through. The more practice you have with improving your vibe while using and regulating energy, the easier you'll be able to engage from a solid, grounded Sense of Self.

Let's explore some ineffective measures you may have taken to manage your energy and emotion. Below is a list of counterproductive habits, thoughts, and patterns that influence your energy, your perspective, the way you approach and interact with people or situations, and the way others experience you. Engaging in any of these on a regular basis creates a negative energy field that impacts you and those around you. Though some of these may be a natural response to stress, fear, difficult feelings, or uncertainty, they can also become habits and trained responses.

LOW-ENERGY VIBES

Judgment	Fear	Blame	Rigidity
Complaining	Hostility	Control	Comparison
Catastrophizing	Frustration	Competition	Criticism
Disappointment	Worry	Rushing	Jealousy
Too Much Effort	Tension	Irritation	Negativity

Habits such as these can be changed with a commitment and diligence to do so. How do you get there? The most critical work before you is to "know thyself." Have the courage to reflect and be honest about the methods you've used to relate and navigate the world. It's important to assess if these strategies are healthy and effective and if they're true to who and how you want to be.

With the right strategies and attentiveness, any of the low-energy vibes can be replaced by the following:

HIGH-ENERGY VIBES

Joy	Wonderment	Curiosity	Gratitude
Ease	Appreciation	Happiness	Laughter
Calm	Enthusiasm	Love	Encouragement
Service	Smiling	Hope	Celebration

We've talked about cleaning up the rubbish in your environment, and now the challenge is to clean up your vibe. Like giving up carbs or sugar, you're going to limit a few of the emotional toxins for a while to see how much better you feel. Each time you notice any of the low-energy vibes, choose a different one from the list above. It's a practice and it may take time, but it's worth it. If fear is gripping at your heels and causing you to awfulize your life or project worst-case scenarios, find something lighter and happier to focus on. Feel that experience in your body. Picture it in your mind. Breathe a high-flying vibe into your body with special focus on your heart. Allow a smile to come across your lips. Remember, slow, steady shifts up the energy scale to improve as much as feels right without forcing or faking it.

WHERE TO BEGIN

When something's troubling you, perhaps someone has suggested, "Just don't think about it." This is probably the most ridiculous advice ever given (particularly when it's given to an Empath). If it were so easy to not think about something, everyone would do it, and there wouldn't be any problems. But the brain can't simply *stop thinking* about something. It's designed to think, and rarely can that same troubled brain effectively think you through a problem. Trying to stop a freight train through sheer resistance or by stepping in front of it is a dangerous feat. Trying to stop the brain from doing its job of thinking isn't particularly effective, especially a riddled brain. However, it is very possible to move out of negative thoughts by *thinking about something else*. Like trying to take candy from a baby, it's much easier when you hand that precious child something else to focus on. So too is the way of that thinking brain.

While proudly sharing a story about her new motorcycle riding skills, Cindy explained that the most helpful input she received from her instructor was, "Where you look is where you go. The motorcycle will move wherever you are focusing." The same is true in life. What are you concentrating on? What are you allowing your mind to focus on? From the moment you wake up, what thoughts and habits are you entertaining?

Concentrating on the negative will expand the negative and feed the downward spiral. You can slow the momentum of this by creating a deliberate focal point for your brain to have something positive to center on. This doesn't have to be hard or monumental. Dismantling your belief systems and thought patterns can be as easy as a simple, steadfast practice of shifting your vibe and lightening your focus and mentality.

If someone in the room were getting sick and you continued to stare, it wouldn't take long for you to feel ill, as that uncomfortable churn in your stomach starts and you sense your lunch now wanting to make a sudden return. If you choose to look away and focus on someone or something else, the feeling goes away because you are now concentrating on something more enjoyable. You can practice this same strategy every time you notice your energy, emotion, or thought declining. All you have to do is focus somewhere else to align with something more enjoyable. Each time you drift back (and you will), gently redirect your focus back to what you were concentrating on.

If you're fatigued by the day, acknowledge something you accomplished. If you're feeling overwhelmed by chores, shift your focus to the blessing of owning a dishwasher and having running water, dishes, and utensils to make eating more manageable; feel the heat of the water and the smell of the soap; or acknowledge having clean clothes to wear and fold them with gratitude. Turn your "have-to" energy into "get-to" or "thank-you-for" energy. If you were ghosted by someone on the first date, offer gratitude that you must've been saved from someone who was not meant for you. If your mood is low, cover up with a blanket you love, turn on some music to lift your spirits, light a candle, and sort through the pile of magazines you've been meaning to get to. Changing your vibration is often as simple as changing your focus and altering the story in your head. Offer your body and brain something else to concentrate on rather than just trying to stop thinking about it.

If you decide that you need a blue shirt, you'll likely walk into a store or search online for blue shirts. You won't spend time on paisley or yellow ones. There's no sense looking at what you don't want, because doing so would be distracting and unproductive. A preference for blue shirts doesn't eliminate or ridicule the others; it simply narrows your focus to what you're looking for. It aligns you with what you want and allows the other choices to fall to the background. The lesson: home in on what you *do* want in life rather than on what you don't, over and over again.

If you're trying to shift low-energy vibes into high-energy vibes, below are a few practices you can never go wrong with.

- Pick an affirmation and repeat it as often as possible. Feel the emotion of it.
- Focus on something that feels good—the sky, a color, soft skin, a fragrance, the flicker of a candle.
- Think about a color you like. Look for it as you go about your day, and use it as a simple spiritual wink or thumbs-up.
- Acknowledge something you're grateful for, no matter how small.
- Call someone you love.
- Find a positive word to concentrate on (words like joy, laughter, worthy).
- Take a breath, feel the expansion of your lungs, and let out a sigh.
- Say a prayer and visualize a release.
- Choose a tarot or oracle card for direction, guidance, or clarity.
- Feel your feet on the ground and send energy down and through your feet.
- Smile, even if you don't feel like it.
- Look in the mirror and into your eyes. Now smile.
- Think about something you're looking forward to.
- Recall a time when you felt really happy.

Feel the energy of these techniques and allow them to resonate in your body, even for a few moments. These practices will alter your energy, outlook, and perspective. They don't deny or minimize what's happening; they simply shift your focus and allow you to concentrate on the things you can control and things that feel good. It's a perspective shift that allows you to alter your state just long enough for there to be some wiggle room in your mindset or mood. It's like loosening a knot.

HOW TO USE ENERGY

Exploring energy can be a playful, fun, and creative endeavor. It can be an amazing way to *feel* your way through life as you incorporate Embodiment, senses, and emotions to explore more deeply. Using different methods to maneuver energy will allow you to regulate it effectively and utilize it as guidance and information to serve you best. The goal of this work is to notice and get curious about what you're experiencing. Like a gift that's presented to you—inquire about it, pick it up, shake it, roll it around, and with a sense of wonderment, see what's inside.

The first step is to detect what you're feeling and where you're experiencing it in your body. Is there an ache in your chest, a change in your breathing, a surge of anxiety? When something is stirring inside of you, inquire and investigate it. What are you feeling? Where are you feeling it? Get curious and spend time exploring what's happening. Is the sensation sharp, jagged, heavy, solid, rigid, firm, squishy, or soft? Can you ascribe a color, temperature, or texture to it? This imagery allows you to explore in a playful, experiential way. Ignite your curiosity and tune in to what you're experiencing, how it feels, and where it gathers in your body.

Next, breathe into the areas of your body where you notice the energy and practice moving it around. Put your hands where you feel it most and breathe in to send light and air to that place inside you. Visualize moving the energy out of your body. You may prefer to move it down and out through your feet, or perhaps to move it out through the top of your head, offering it to the sky or to your God. Alternately, you could envision a surge out of your chest like a big puff of smoke.

Visualization is a fun, creative way to explore what works for you. It is most effective and productive when you play with different techniques in varying circumstances to assess what you need the most. The only critical factor is that you move the energy out to avoid it becoming stuck or clogged within you.

Here are a few ways to add variety to your visualizations:

- Imagine energy being connected to a switch that you can access at any point, like a light switch you turn off and on as needed.
  - As you lie down for bed at night, turn off the switch to allow a good night's sleep, knowing you can turn it back on in the morning.
  - If you're at your kid's sporting event, keep the switch off until the game is over, and resume when the time is right by switching it back on.
  - If you're ruminating about a particularly difficult interaction with someone, envision an off switch as you disengage from them. If thoughts or feelings start to arise, remind yourself that the lights are off on that issue, and it is over for the day.
- Visualize a dial that regulates the amount of energy you are allowing yourself to absorb. Just like you turn down the volume on your music for a softer setting, you can also experiment with lowering the amount of energy you allow in.

- If you feel flooded by an experience, imagine turning the dial to quiet the noise or to dull the intensity of something.

- If you're experiencing emotion at a level ten, decide on a more appropriate "volume" of how you want to feel. Then, turn the dial to a four (for instance) and envision a less intense version of what's happening.

- Imagine yourself boxing things up as you leave one interaction and move into the next. Compartmentalization is a coping mechanism where you "put things away" or divide them into sections or categories.

  - If something is particularly challenging for you, put it in a box on a shelf until the time is right to deal with it.

  - If something wakes you up in the middle of the night, picture putting it back on the shelf where it will be waiting for you in the morning.

- Picture a long tube attached to your body. When dealing with a stressful situation, intense emotion, or conflictual energy, imagine all of it filtering down and out of the tube rather than into you. The tube allows you to be present in a difficult situation or with challenging people without absorbing any of it into you.

- Imagine roots coming out of your feet. You can assign a color, texture, and depth to these roots to explore different grounding or releasing techniques.

  - If you're feeling particularly unsteady about something, imagine deep scarlet ropes traveling miles down into the earth to allow you to stabilize.

○ If you're experiencing a lot of stress and overwhelm, imagine golden roots planted where you can send all of that emotional intensity to be reused and recycled for the sake of good.

These tools will benefit you most when you're creative, playful, and willing to lighten up and explore a bit. None of this needs to be taken very seriously, and the more fun you have with it, the more easily your focus and energy will shift.

FORCE

With hard work and effort, you can achieve anything.

—ANTOINE GRIEZMANN

Determine never to be idle. No person will have occasion to complain of the want of time, who never loses any. It is wonderful how much may be done if we are always doing.

—THOMAS JEFFERSON

If you believe in yourself and have dedication and pride—and never quit, you'll be a winner. The price of victory is high but so are the rewards.

—BEAR BRYANT

Have you ever played tug-of-war? Digging your heels fiercely into the ground, pulling with all your might, the seething pain of the rope burning your hands until that final face-plant as you wipe the dirt from your eyes? Who ever thought that was fun?

Hard work, focus, and drive are necessary ingredients when you're passionate about accomplishing something. There's a time and place for fortitude and grit. Late nights, coffee-stained notes, and vehement conversation about things you're excited about can be great stuff with the right energy.

Yet, we live in a society that prioritizes a single road to success linked to hard work and sacrifice. Our world teaches and reinforces messages about effort, determination, and willpower being the sole road to success. The grindstone mentality of sacrifice, struggle, and vigor is a prerequisite to success and happiness.

If you've drunk the Kool-Aid of faulty beliefs that success is achieved only with hard work and sacrifice—the no pain, no gain mentality—I'll encourage you to question the truth and effectiveness of those beliefs. Why does this have to be the case? Can this truly be the only path to success? Where did you learn that? And why do you continue to buy into it? When did that become fact and *truth*?

Though this commonly accepted mentality is valued and has its place when it comes to accomplishment, it might also lead you to misinterpret obstacles, "failure," and struggles as the need to work harder, the idea that you're doing something wrong, or the tendency to please or appease more. You run the risk of imposing self-will and forcing solutions that may not be in your best interest. This mentality, along with practices such as these, can be counterproductive and misaligned with where you're meant to go in life. It's not likely that you've been taught a balance of using hard work and determination in conjunction with softer, more intricate dynamics that can be far more effective at propelling you into success.

You may battle life and be in a constant tug-of-war with the guidance and direction life is trying to offer you because you've bought into the pressure to do more and work harder. You may have a harsh perspective of success, accomplishment, and achievement tied tightly to your worth and capabilities. Some of these beliefs and patterns may be a result of your own thinking and learning, but they may also be a result of generations of misinformation and misunderstanding.

Can you imagine a blossom exerting itself to bloom, or the sun fraught about whether it will rise every morning? Picture a baby elephant obsessing about its legs and trunk to ensure they develop big and strong enough to perform the tasks of the savannah. Children might never grow, talk, or walk if they bought into the fallacy that living needs to be hard, and that only constant effort will enable them to develop and mature. Nature evolves all on its own, in its own way and time. Somehow, it all takes beautiful care of itself. There is a natural ease that promotes the organic development of a spectacular ecosystem without the frantic attempts for any of nature to *make* something happen.

With the right balance of effort and ease, the same can be true for your personal development and success.

FLOW

Despite what you might have learned, there is a different mindset, one that's often overlooked and undervalued. This mindset draws a distinct line between self-will and the will of something higher, something grander. It's the delicate balance between fear versus faith or Force versus Flow.

Recall the childhood nursery rhyme "Row, Row, Row Your Boat." I ask you to bring it to mind because it's a perfect antidote to the life lessons of Force and effort. You're called to row *gently* down the stream, allowing life to merrily unfold in the dream it is intended to be. It's a tune most of us learned, and yet never thought to apply it to life.

Are you someone who moves gently down the stream of life, or do you fight the current to get things to go the way you want them to? Do you pay attention to the direction life offers, or are you constantly trying to dictate the course and the pace? Are you open and willing to learn, seek guidance, and input, or are you self-determined, always thinking you know best? Do you view obstacles and struggles as information and redirection, or do you interpret them as failures requiring more effort and Force? Are you trusting the Flow of things, or are you adamant and resistant, determined to get life to go your way?

On the other end of the spectrum, have you hopelessly surrendered your efforts and are simply allowing yourself to drift through life? Have you let the paddles go, believing you have no say or influence over life's course? Have you refused to get in the boat altogether and even try to navigate a path?

Nature is the perfect illustration of ease and effortlessness. When it is time, the buds of a flower gently unfold into their own magnificence. When a fetus is finally ready to make her arrival, so many majestic things happen in awe-inspiring ways to move that child into the world. Though hard work and exertion take place, it is the prompt of nature that allows these conditions to occur. Later, when that same child is ready, she speaks her first words or takes her first steps, sending waves of exhilaration to everyone around. She is not ready until the moment she is ready, and once she is, there's no stopping her.

There is a delicate balance between Force and Flow in which you row down the stream, take action, and apply effort as needed, gently. Flow is the beautiful alignment of timing, readiness, and action that allows circumstances to unfold, revealing the next step to be taken. Just as the road rises to meet you exactly where you are, so too does life. There is a gentleness and ease that synchronizes with commitment, effort, and determination in which you pick up the oars and begin to row. There is an organic sweet spot reflecting the nature of Flow, and the more you recognize it, the easier it will be to get and stay in it.

Flow has a certain feel to it and includes things such as coincidence, chances, alignment, synchronicities, feelings, intuition, nudges, gut sense, and miracles. A practice such as this may be counterintuitive and contradict every life lesson you were ever taught. Some people mistake the ease and effortlessness of Flow as lazy, irresponsible, or not enough. It may be diminished or dismissed because its simplicity is underestimated and misunderstood. If Flow has been misrepresented and you feel plagued by the messages of Force, you may completely missing the gift and guidance life has to offer.

Flow is magical and inviting as it opens you to an entirely different realm of possibility. Using the guidance of Flow to know when to rest, take action, wait, or take the leap will offer insight and opportunities you might otherwise miss because you're so focused on trying to Force things into place, accomplish the goal, and achieve the next thing. The distinction between effort and ease is a critical awareness point in learning to navigate Flow.

Flow is accompanied by a trust and an alignment that allows you to be directed and shown something bigger than logic, habits, and rigidity. Flow supports you with inspiration, impulse, nudges, synchronicities, coincidences, whims, and intuitive ideas. A call comes out of nowhere; a chance meeting occurs; an opportunity presents itself; you run into an old friend who just happens to know someone they want to introduce you to; the check comes in the mail; you experience an instinctual nudge informing you that it's time to take action on the plan you've put on hold. That's Flow steering you where you need to go.

FREE FALL

Have you ever done a trust fall? Where did that foolish idea come from? Isn't it a crazy thing? You willingly let go, fall backward, and trust that someone is going to catch you. You volunteer for that! The courage and trust this requires is astounding!

A consistent practice of Flow can feel very much like a free fall in the beginning, the perception that you're falling into an abyss of uncertainty and submission. Surrender can be a terrifying concept, especially if you're used to Force energy and are operating under those faulty beliefs and misperceptions. If you're mistaking the powerful spiritual stance of Flow as lackadaisical, not enough, or failure, I assure you, it is not.

Hardship, heartache, and struggles can leave you hurt, confused, and distrusting of anyone or anything. If you learned the suck-it-up, nose-to-the-grindstone approach to success and well-being, falling safely into the arms of life can feel frightening and confusing. You may mistake surrender with helplessness or careless efforts. Letting go of the illusion of control and the rigid energy of Force can feel like a slip into an endless abyss. You may feel irresponsible or lazy if you're not constantly striving or putting forth some sort of effort. Quite the contrary.

Flow is the practice of tuning in to the ease and direction toward which life is pointing you. It is an intuitive nudge that encourages you to make the call, accept the invite, register for the conference, ask him for coffee. Courageous spurts of excitement and curiosity will encourage you to go in a certain direction or take a specific action. There is no pursuing, chasing, forcing, or *making* something happen.

Flow is directly linked to your intuition, that wise part of you that always seems to *know*. It requires a deep-seated trust. Imagine a turtle tucked safely within its protective shell, awaiting calm and quiet before peeking out. Any detection of chaos or pandemonium will cause the turtle to recoil and wait for its next opportunity to surface. So it is with the intuition. Too much commotion or stress will drown out the tranquil nature of it. Like a friendly visitor, it will rarely barge in. Intuition will await your invitation and patience before entering. Create and allow conditions and practices for the intuition to come forth. Recognize its gentle knock as you learn to listen and tune in to it where you're being guided.

Flow feels different for everyone. At first, it may be easier to recognize when you're out of it with the common symptoms of frustration, overwhelm, and uncertainty. Noticing these emotions and energetic states will provide important information that it may be time to rest, reflect, and reset.

Take the time to assess and clarify your understanding of and approach to success and accomplishment. If you have faulty beliefs and attitudes, it's important to clean them up and realign them with what's in your best interest. This basic foundation allows you to cultivate an amazing relationship with your intuition as you develop a deep-seated trust that life will guide, protect, and direct you toward your highest and best. Your well-practiced belief systems and outlook will define your slant on life. If you personalize struggle and hardship, force solutions, or deem yourself or your efforts as failures or mistakes, you've bought into the lie and pressures of Force. When you choose to see obstacles and complications as guidance and information that need your attention and reflection, you've begun to work in alignment with life and intuition to create the perfect conditions for Flow.

GENTLY DOWN THE STREAM

Have you ever seen the driver who dangerously pushes traffic, dodges in and out of slower-paced cars, and rides your tail, only to wind up next to you at the light? What's your reaction to interactions like that? Pause for a moment of honesty: Are *you* that driver? Do you take the same approach to life, believing you have to force your will, your plan, your agenda, and time frame or else you'll never get anywhere? Do you try to move others along, believing you have to *make* things happen?

Every time you get in the car, you probably have an idea of where you're headed. However, it's not likely you're trying to predict, manipulate, and control every inch of the road that lies ahead. Despite your best efforts, you can't push traffic or force conditions to be different than they are. You can try to maneuver in and around things in an effort to get somewhere. You can wait patiently or impatiently. You can even decide it's not worth it and turn around and go home. You can extend as much or as little effort as you see fit, and you can take any attitude or approach you'd like. But you can't make the trip unfold any faster than it's intended to.

An alternative: you can trust the road as it unfolds, adjusting yourself accordingly, knowing that you will arrive, eventually, at the exact place you're meant to be.

It's important to recognize the energy of Force—with its harried nature of frenzy, fury, and figuring out—early in the process, as this allows you to reassess and realign your efforts sooner rather than later. Forty miles into the trip, it's frustrating and disappointing to realize that you need to reroute. You ignored the signs and now need to double back with the sunk costs of time, energy, and effort. Doing this four miles into the trip is much more manageable and realistic. The sooner you recognize the energy and effort you're putting forth, the sooner you'll be able to recognize misalignment.

If you tend to force and control life, if you ignore or override obstacles and delays, or you unwaveringly stick to an agenda that's not working, you are in a Force mindset. This is your wake-up call to pay attention to what you're doing and how hard you're pushing. Force is rigid, vigorous, and controlling. Flow, meanwhile, loosens your grip on outcomes, time frames, and agendas to open you to possibilities and alternatives that are in your best interest, even when you can't see it. You see only a portion of the picture that's viewed from your own perspective. There is a Source that sees a much bigger picture, knows all the right players, and recognizes the importance of divine timing with all the people involved. Flow allows you to step out of Force with all of its rigidity, limitation, habits, and trained thoughts, and affords you a much greater perspective, and plan to accomplish whatever it is you've been trying to accomplish.

Mark recently got wind of an entrepreneurial project but only agreed to the terms and conditions because of the continuous prompting of the father-in-law he always tried to impress. He immediately got to work, buying into the notion that chances like this don't come around often. That was the leading line of every conversation he'd had with his father-in-law for weeks. He dove in headfirst, not wanting to give the other guy (or lady, whoever he or she may be) a chance to steal this opportunity away—particularly since the opportunity, in his mind, was also a chance to finally win the acceptance and approval of his wife's father. So, he quickly got busy gathering information, setting up meetings and late-night calls, accessing funds, and establishing the course as he pushed forth. He set the agenda, time frame, and outcomes he thought he should achieve. The venture soon took up every ounce of energy, conversation, and finance he had.

Early on, there were signs that something wasn't right. Within days, obstacles began cropping up. Things seemed to go wrong, delays set in, documents got lost, and unexpected fees and expenses crept in. There was a nagging sense that kept him up at night and caused anxiety like he'd never felt before—not minor frustrations, but huge issues associated with programming, large debt, website hijacking, fraudulent information, and misinformation from a shady investor.

"That's the price of success; you've got to spend money to make money," boomed the voices inside his head. "This is a chance of a lifetime. You have to chase after it, no matter what it costs."

So he ignored, downplayed, and chastised the part of him that was tired, cautious, and trying to heed warning. He was consumed, exhausted, and depleted but had way too much to do and was way too worried about what other people thought to pay attention to how he felt.

Hours and days ticked away while the dollar signs added up far too quickly. One crisis after another continued to surface, but Mark had learned the lessons about sacrifice, perfectionism, hard work, and determination. He could hear the echoing voice of his successful father: "Nothing worth having comes easy, son."

Mark wasn't afraid of hard work, but the scales had tipped long ago, and he and everyone around him were now paying the price. He sat day and night at his computer, canceled plans and family vacations, took a loan against the house without his wife's knowledge, missed recitals, birthday parties, and holidays because of the pressure and panic associated with this project he *had* to accomplish. Stress levels skyrocketed. The effort level was intense and relentless.

It was after one final face-plant experience that Mark finally let go of the rope. With a resounding sense of failure and defeat, he stepped back to assess two years of tug-of-war damage and the devastating effects that occurred. It was overwhelming for him to survey the consequences of his behavior and choices, especially when he thought he'd been doing the right thing, doing what he *should* to build wealth and success.

Mark landed in my office to help sort through the rubble. Grief and embarrassment were two of the leading emotions he had to sort through. His work first centered around awareness and coming to terms with the reality of what he had created. He then began unwinding beliefs and mindsets as well as dismantling habits, routines, behaviors, and patterns about building success, establishing wealth, and being a man and a provider. His people-pleasing and perfectionism patterns, along with secrecy and lies of omission, were hard for him to deal with without going to shame and failure-mode. Mark had been molded, like most of us, into the grindstone mentality of Force, and it had cost him and his family greatly.

It took months for Mark to learn to make room for his emotions and understand the concept of Flow. He had to experiment with it and get the feel of it. He had to learn how to tune in to his senses, energy, and emotion about things as he learned to quiet the mind chatter and recognize his intuition. Like developing a routine to build muscle slowly and steadily, Mark began to focus on small victories. Coincidences and synchronicities that he would've previously overlooked as trivial or chalked up to happenstance now became the highlights of his day and the topic of conversations. Gut feelings that he used to suppress and deny soon became his messengers and advocates.

Mark always thought he knew best, and that strong will and determination would land him where he needed to be if he just worked harder and stuck with it long enough. Those two grindstone years humbled him and left a lot of wreckage, but he began to understand the brute force of his ego and will. He softened, and his perspective changed as he learned to recognize the egoic drive of Force. Ease and enjoyment were new to him too as he learned to trust the process, tune in to obstacles and the information they were offering, and embrace and assess circumstances without rigidity, fear, or control.

During our Tuesday appointment, Mark excitedly plopped down on the couch and reported a series of events that unfolded in the most unexpected ways now that he recognized Flow. A long, winding story revealed some of the craziest details about a series of events that boiled down to being late for a critical meeting because he got trapped in an elevator for over ninety minutes. What once would've sent him into a reactionary state of Force was now seen as an opportunity to witness and assess circumstances just long enough to feel for potential Flow. At this point, he'd learned that life directs and redirects until we pay attention to where it's pointing.

He told the story of making his way to an interview one morning, and though he would typically take the stairs, he felt an intuitive nudge to hop on the elevator. He almost overrode the compulsion but had committed to honor those whimsical impulses. He slid his way through the doors that were just about to close and nodded politely at the gentleman positioned in the back as he pressed the button for the tenth floor.

Just a few moments into the ride, Mark felt a sudden jolt as the elevator screeched to a halt. Confusion, panic, and desperation flooded him as his mind began to race and envision disaster. He paused, then forcefully pressed the buttons to remind the elevator it should be moving along, all to no avail. He looked hopelessly at the gentleman behind him as he experienced the old energy of fear, frustration, and anxiety.

"Hold on a minute," he said to himself as he established his breath and captured his thoughts. Mark had been learning the energy of Flow, and so he knew that things happen for a reason. So, he got himself centered and grounded as he took a breath and mustered some awkward but friendly conversation with the gentleman. A situation he previously would've seen as tragic, frustrating, a mistake, an accident, or a mishap that would've sent him into a fury was now being used as information, guidance, and direction. The two gentlemen chatted about random things, trying to keep their minds off the danger and risk. They spoke about family, children, firemen, childhood dreams, baseball, and the discomfort of small spaces. They offered one another assurance, respect, and small doses of humor.

Just as suddenly as it had stopped, the elevator jolted back into action and made its ascension to the tenth floor. The two men didn't speak another word, simply shook hands and offered a nod of the head as they both exited. Mark headed for suite 1010 and laughed as the other man entered the same office.

The woman behind the counter anxiously glanced at the clock that was nearing 11:15. "Good morning, Mr. Hansen," she exclaimed. "We've been waiting for you. But no worries, your first appointment never arrived."

Once again, the two elevator companions' eyes met, and the two men laughed as though they found themselves in the front row of the best comedy act they'd ever seen.

"You're right, Elizabeth," the other man said. "No worries at all. It appears the universe had other intentions for our meeting this morning. I'd like you to meet . . ." He paused, realizing he and his elevator companion had never introduced themselves.

"Mark. I'm Mark." He shook the hand of the very polite but confused woman.

A job offer came within two days, and Mark was to start the following Monday with a salary, bonus structure, and travel options that were beyond anything he could've imagined for himself. His voice quivered as he shared the details with me. He seemed to be in awe of the events, the ease and nature of how they had transpired, especially after the grueling efforts he had been consumed by for those two long, stressful years of trying to Force a failing business to succeed.

"It was the nudge," he said humbly. "I would've taken the stairs before had I not listened to the nudge. I never would've let myself stand still for a three-minute elevator ride. It was the nudge."

Of course, Mark's is a story of magic, simplicity, coincidence, circumstance, and ease. It's a story of intuition, guidance, trust, and tuning in. Every step of the way, Mark was being directed and shown, and when he was in Force mode, those signs and indicators were dismissed, overlooked, and overridden. He saw clearly how his old patterns would've ruined the entire experience, or perhaps they wouldn't have allowed it to happen at all. He felt guided, cared for, and deeply trusting as he took his next step in learning the guidance and assistance of Flow.

THE ENERGY OF FLOW

To have faith is to trust yourself to the water. When you swim you don't grab hold of the water, because if you do you will sink and drown. Instead you relax, and float.

—ALAN WATTS

Like your favorite recipe requires specific ingredients, Flow also relies on precise elements. Below are some components that allow you to recognize when you're in Flow and when you've fallen out.

- **Fluidity**—Think of water with its natural movement of elegance and grace flowing easily from one place to another. The movement is effortless, yet distinct and determined. Flow is an energized force that's fluid, easy, and, light.

- **Fun**—You know you're in Flow when you're having so much fun you don't want to stop. There's laughter, excitement, and joy associated with what you're doing and who you're with. You look forward to things, prioritize them, and feel happy when you partake.

- **Focus**—Have you ever been so lost in something that you lose track of time? You forget to look at the clock because you just love what you're doing and feel so good doing it? That's the focus associated with Flow. You become so absorbed and concentrated on your task that other things don't matter as much. There's passion and enthusiasm with what you're doing, and you'd love to do it all day long. Your conversations and thoughts continue to drift back to your passion, while excitement and enthusiasm drive you.

- **Flexibility**—Imagine water hitting an obstacle, the way it naturally adjusts itself to glide its way around. Obstacles, road-blocks, and challenges don't have to be the end of the road for you. They're simply pieces of information to pay attention to. Are you being called to move differently, go in another direction, wait a while longer, go left when you were heading right? Readjusting and realigning yourself, your thoughts, or your actions will support the supple nature of Flow. Life will direct you to specific things, and any type of hindrance is offering you guidance. Stay flexible and fluid without losing your passion and focus.

- **Forward motion**—Flow produces momentum and movement. You don't stay still for long unless you're in a season of waiting, and even still, there's excitement, passion, and alignment. There will be coincidences and synchronicities you'll recognize if you're paying attention. Someone you thought about last week will suddenly call; you'll have a "chance" meeting in the hallway with the exact contact you're looking for; the money will show up; an intuitive whisper will make you jump out of bed; a conversation will spark a flood of ideas and inspiration. Forward motion is magnetizing and energetic. Be mindful of goals and time frames without getting rigid and locked in.

- **Faith**—This is the single most important factor in allowing Flow. Faith supports your passion beyond hard times, doubt, mishaps, logic, frustration, or criticism. It is complete trust, a *knowing* that you're on the right path, that you have purpose in life, that you're being guided even when things are taking a long time or have resulted in numerous detours. Faith brings confidence and assurance that goes beyond proof and facts. You just *know* and you act accordingly, trusting that you're working in perfect alignment with a deeper purpose and plan.

Here are a few more factors that will help you recognize Flow:

Authenticity	Joy	Alignment	Curiosity
Satisfaction	Passion	Productivity	Spontaneity
Appreciation	Gratitude	Service	Generosity
Transparency	Ease	Humor	Fun
Concentration	Creativity	Rewarding	Motivation
Endless Ideas	Enjoyment	Clarity	Epiphany

These are high-flying vibes that will support you as you move gently down the stream. You can't go wrong with incorporating any of these principles into your daily life. These are words and energy fields you can practice and concentrate on to stay motivated, realign your priorities, and serve as a powerful reset. The more you practice them, the easier they become.

THE ENERGY OF FORCE

Force is the antithesis of Flow. It contains effort and energy that's like rowing upstream. It's the tendency to push your agenda, time frame, and outcomes with striving, dictating, and extending tremendous effort, often resulting in what I refer to as Trying Too Hard (TTH) energy. Force is rigid, exhausting, and you're not getting anywhere without a constant push. You pull the reins so tightly with unyielding focus and fierce determination, pinching off ease, enjoyment, curiosity, and wonderment. Your view is limited and your approach is rigid, so possibilities are restricted.

Force can be defined by its inflexible, coercive exertion. It is an intense, no-holds-barred approach that allows no room for guidance, input, or redirection. Most likely, the approach is based on your will, plan, and timing, and you spend a lot of energy and effort enforcing the "right" course of action for yourself and everyone else. You work hard to orchestrate things to get them the way you think they need to be, and you believe anything else is failure, a mistake, or a waste.

Let's be clear: Force is not to be confused with hard work or determination. There can be tremendous work and effort in Flow, but there's a very different feel to it. When you're in Flow, you're moving along, are happy, and others aren't running the other way when you walk into a room. Force is furious and vigorous and not in your best interest. You'll recognize it quickly once you become familiar with the way it feels and the ease you experience.

Ingredients associated with Force:

- **Fear**—At the heart of most dysfunction and disruption is fear. You're concerned that something will happen or won't happen, the timing won't be right, the money won't be there, someone will leave, or maybe they'll stay . . . So, you try to make sure things go the way you think they should go. Being driven by fear and making decisions from that place will alter your perspective and ability to trust and tune in to your intuition. Fear is anxious and panicky; intuition is soft and subtle. Fear is a terrible motivator and attractor.
  - ○ Intuition doesn't want to work in the face of fear any more than you do. It will wait until the fear subsides.

- **Figuring Out**—You're in your head, constantly trying to strategize, devise a plan, or stay ten steps ahead. You try to make sense of things and take only a logical approach. Figuring out severs you from intuition, body, and senses. You tackle life like it's a chess game, constantly assessing your moves and the moves of others.
  - ○ Intuition is a trust and knowing, not the feverish energy of figuring out.

- **Frenzy**—Your attempts lack focus and direction. There's an intensity to what you're doing, but you struggle to collect your thoughts or launch plans and ideas because you don't have clarity, discipline, or concentration on what you're trying to achieve.

- o Intuition will avoid the whirlwind energy of frenzy and wait for calm to arrive.

- **Freak Out**—You are riddled with high emotion, often presenting as distress or anxiety. Irritability and impatience are no stranger to this frequency. There's a rushed, chaotic element to what you're doing, and the intensity is distracting and counterproductive.
  - o Intuition is grounded and assured, and steers clear of this drama and chaos. It functions best with a sense of calm and moderation.

- **Fear of Missing Out (FOMO)**—Life, success, love, and happiness are not pies. If someone gets a slice—even a really big slice—of the pie, there's still plenty available for you. Life does not run out of blessings or opportunities. You won't miss out on things that are meant for you. If something happens in which you perceive you're missing out, that is fear rearing its ugly head.
  - o Intuition recognizes that if something is intended for you, it will cross your path and make itself available to you. A deep-seated trust in this belief will instantly align with Flow and allow you to tune in to the intuition.

- **Fury / Fight**—You argue with the reality of life and have a spirit of resistance and anger. You focus on the way you think things *should* be rather than on the way they are. Maybe things haven't gone your way, or you've come from the school of hard knocks, but you've got an edge about you. You won't back down to anyone for anything, and there is a sense of intolerance, rigidity, annoyance, or impatience.

- Just as the turtle waits for calm before it peeks its head, intuition will do the same. You cannot attract what you want with hostile, defensive energy.

- **Fake**—Most Empaths can't stand phonies. Like a dog who can instantly track a scent, Empaths can sniff out fake energy quite easily. However, as an Empath, you may have a tendency to please and perform in which you're not grounded in authenticity and personal truth. You may prioritize the feelings and needs of others and lose touch with what's in your best interest. If you're behaving in ways that are not true to you or trying to accomplish something you feel you *should* be doing or that's misaligned with who you really are or what you want, that superficial energy will come through. If you've learned to go along to get along or you don't know how to assert yourself, you may have faked your way through life.
  - Intuition knows nothing but your true self and will not allow anything disingenuous.

- **Flooding**—Thoughts flying, restless energy, sleepless nights, and hurried speech and ideas are all symptoms of flooding. Rushing, overwhelm, or deluging are counterproductive to Flow. This isn't the best place to determine your next steps or make decisions from, though waiting or doing nothing may instinctively feel wrong or lazy. Flooding may require time to allow things to settle and shake out to see what needs your attention and what doesn't.

- o Intuition is smooth, natural movement, and momentum without the overwhelm of flooding.

- **Fatigue**—Weariness, exhaustion, and lethargy are indicators for rest. The mind, body, and spirit all work best when properly refueled and can recoup from the hustle and bustle with proper sleep, downtime, and relaxation. Rest and leisure are not wasted time; they're necessary.
  - o Intuition will come most easily during times of sleep and stillness because you're not caught up in the frenzied chaos of the world.

- **Frustration**—Moving upstream is exhausting, and frustration is an important cue indicating overexertion, misalignment, and self-will. It's like the rumble strips on the side of the road that warn that you've moved off course. Frustration is trying to alert you to something that needs to be redirected or perhaps you're trying too hard (TTH) to make something happen in a time or way it's not meant to happen.
  - o There's enjoyment, productivity, and ease to intuition.

- **Fed-upness**—You've waited too long to pay attention to feelings, cues, and indicators for realignment. If you're exhausted, empty, and resentful from all the hard work and effort you've put forth, you may be totally fed up with people and situations. If you haven't been honoring your commodities of time, energy, and effort, it may have led you to a very worn-out place.

o Intuition requires emotional stability so it can assure your well-being and readiness before it guides you along your path.

Here are some additional cues that further indicate Force:

Scarcity / Lack	Striving	Rigidity	Cynicism
Imposter Syndrome	Resistance	Refusal	Rumination
Comparison	Proving	Perfecting	Pleasing
Locking in on outcomes	Confusion	Rushing	Unyielding
Forcing solutions	Disruption	Distraction	Chaos

These signs and symptoms offer important information and are indicators of misalignment, self-will, and contaminated energy. Each of these leave energetic residue, and cause wear and tear to the mind, body, and intuition. The more you practice the ease and simplicity of Flow, the sooner you'll recognize when you have stepped out of it. As you begin to drift into the counterproductive zone of Force, somatic symptoms and emotions will alert you and call for a reset and realignment. Like the disruptive jolt of those roadside strips, the ingredients of Force will awaken you so you can quickly realign with Flow.

WHERE TO BEGIN

Reset: Awareness is an incredible tool and a critical starting point. Yet, you can be aware of something with no idea what to do or how to manage it. The leap between Force and Flow may feel like a big one, but I assure you, minor shifts and adjustments will do a lot to realign you with Flow.

It's important to catch the symptoms of Force in their early stages. Any indication of Force is a cue for a mental, physical, or energetic check-in to see where things went off the rails. The sooner you practice this and the earlier you detect the symptoms, the quicker you can intervene.

The prefix "re" means back or again. How often when you lose something do you retrace your steps to find the lost item, or you're not satisfied with a task, so you redo it? If you've ever lost your balance, have you taken a moment to restabilize yourself? When a contract is not to your liking, are there terms and conditions you renegotiate? You get the concept! It's life's opportunity for a do-over.

There are times we need to be in the energy of "re"—a willingness to go back, to try again. This is some of the wisest, most solid navigation you'll ever accomplish. Force is not bad, failure, or something you've done wrong; it's energy. And it's counterproductive. Just like you're practicing gently shifting emotions up the energetic scale, so too can you shift the patterns of Force. As soon as you recognize the symptoms of this ineffective path, call it out, name it so you can reestablish your footing and assess your next right steps.

Reset Practices:

Refocus—It's easy to get off track and lose focus on what you're doing and why you're doing it. Before you know it, you're drifting off course and maneuvering away from your goals. When you notice these patterns, it's helpful to refocus your efforts and priorities to help you gain clarity and momentum. What's your purpose? What's important to you? What's your *why* for doing this project? What are your core values? Who do you want to be in the world? Get crystal clear of your mission and purpose so you can get back on track.

Reassess—This is your ability to evaluate what you're doing and the quality of your efforts. It allows you to take stock and decide what's working and what isn't and any changes that need to be made. It's an updated perspective as you've gotten further down the road and a chance to consider new information. There are many variables to consider that influence your journey and what priorities need to be established. Reassessing is your ability to navigate change, choose your resources and assets, and redirect wherever needed.

Redefine—Could you imagine subscribing to the guidelines of kindergarten? Of course not! With age comes experience and wisdom, and more is revealed. As you grow, change, mature, and gain knowledge, your perspective, outlook, needs, and capabilities also change. At any point, you can alter terms and conditions, expectations, what you're doing, why and how you're doing it. You can take an issue or concept down to the studs and consider carefully what's important to you, what you need, and what works for you. You can ask for what you want, orchestrate and design tasks, conversations, situations, and relationships or just about anything you're engaged in. Just because you always have, doesn't mean you always will. You can assess and redefine at any point.

Redo—Don't be afraid to start over again. There is wisdom, experience, and knowledge you'll bring with you this time that you didn't have the first time. A willingness to scrap the whole thing often sets the foundation as a propellent into the next level of success and achievement. Redoing a task, conversation, or project is simply a powerful reset to get things the way you feel is best.

The childlike energy of getting a redo can be the exact opportunity you need for a fresh start.

Renegotiate—As an Empath, you may have a hard time with decisions, choices, conversation, assertion, and confrontation. Yet, what was once acceptable may no longer be, and it is time to discuss and reconsider. Things are rarely written in stone, so you can decide to take things back to the drawing board to renegotiate terms and conditions that are easier, healthier, and more productive for you.

Reclaim—To claim something is to call it your own. As an Empath, you may have lost touch with yourself and what's important to you. Reclaiming yourself—your purpose, goals, vision, worth, or focus is an empowering certainty and assertion. Sometimes it's as easy as a decision. You recognize the value and importance of something, so you draw a line in the sand and claim it as yours. If things have gotten a little too far out of reach, if others are influencing your decisions and perspective, you may need to reclaim your personal power and vision. Own it and take it as yours with a determined sense of accomplishment and purpose.

Regroup—Making your dreams come true and living your life purpose can feel overwhelming and even burdensome at times. Having passion and purpose does not mean the road will be smooth and easy. Maybe the long trudge forward has left you a little out of whack, exhausted, and misaligned. It's okay to rest and reassemble your resources, stamina, and energy. Take a breath, celebrate your wins, and rejuvenate as you gather yourself for your next steps.

Redecide—This is perhaps my favorite. As adults, we have the gift of free will and personal responsibility. At any point, you can make up your mind or change your mind, and you can do so as many times as you need to. How often have you gotten further into something and thought, *This isn't what I thought it was going to be?* How often do others not live up to their end of the deal, yet you feel the obligation to carry the entire thing? Life sometimes offers obstacles and challenges to direct you down a different path, so you need to reroute your decisions and efforts. Redeciding is not failure. It's a necessary tool to recenter you back into Flow.

There is a sense of gentleness, allowing, permission, and compassion in each of these steps. These are beautifully aligned with the ease and safety of Flow. Consistent permission to use any of these "re" steps helps you realize you cannot fail, there are no mistakes, and everything is an opportunity to practice, learn, grow, and try. It allows one of the most important "re" practices, which is reassurance.

TIPS AND TOOLS FOR USING EMOTION AND ENERGY TO BE IN FLOW

- **Breath is life.** Of course, you do it all the time, but being deliberate about using breath in your energetic practices enables you to use this life force in powerful ways. Learn to use it in different capacities to release emotion, stimulate energy, move tension, ground yourself, connect with spirit, etc. A deep, cathartic breath can be a mighty release and reset. It can shift your energy quickly and effectively. Rapid, repetitive breath can stimulate and activate thought, emotion, and energy. Slow, steady breath can calm, soothe, and regulate you. Breath is your essential tool for energy management and regulation. Use it intentionally to direct and manage your thoughts, emotion, and energy. Dr. Sue Morter offers a great example of this in the powerful practice of central channel breathing.

- **Be in and around water as much as you can.** Not only is it a sacred element, it's also a perfect illustration of Flow. Listen to it; witness its beauty and effortlessness; put your hands, feet, or entire body in it. Recognize how smoothly water navigates around obstacles and tune in to elements of ease. Use the simple acts of washing your hands or showering as ways to experience the nurturance, cleansing, and grounding of water.

- **Be still.** Create time and space for rest, calm, and quiet so you can open yourself to Spirit and intuitive nudges. Intuition speaks quietly and subtly, and stillness allows you to hear more clearly and recognize your inner voice, emotions, and bodily senses. Busyness, distraction, and lack of focus will misalign and clog you. Stillness promotes and allows the energy of Flow.

- **Be mindful of the ways certain people, places, and things influence your energy.** Pay attention to how you feel and what you experience. Create relationships and experiences that fuel you and fill your cup, not drain it. Who's positive and fun to be around? Who stimulates good conversation? What makes you feel good, inspires, and supports you? Where do you feel calm, content, and comfortable? Spend time there.

- **Use each of your senses and all parts of your body.** Have a consistent Embodiment practice of movement, sensory awareness, and breath work to fully incorporate your entire being in experiencing and moving emotion and energy.

- **Pay attention to your thoughts, feelings, and reactions to understand and appreciate energy.** Recognize how you can use positive words, thoughts, feelings, and behaviors to align with Flow more effectively. Think about what you're thinking about and have deliberate methods for improving your thoughts and energy levels.

- **Learn to distinguish the qualities and conditions of Flow to keep yourself within its navigational beams.** Pay attention to where life is trying to take you and when things are moving along smoothly. If something isn't working, frustration is mounting, or doors keep closing, life may be trying to point you in a different direction. Awareness and acceptance are critical factors in letting go of outcomes and trusting the process to realign with Flow.

- **Stay open to alternatives.** Some of the best options open when you allow yourself to consider a Plan B. Flow is notorious for rerouting when it sees a better path that will serve you more effectively. Flow sees the opportunities from a perspective you may not be able to see and wants to guide you there. Keep an open mind and be flexible without bending too much and getting too far off course. Learn to trust the process, adapt when necessary, and shift gears without compromising yourself and your values.

- **Develop a deep-seated belief that life has your back and is working in your favor.** Esther Hicks is a spiritual speaker who often quotes the powerful mantra, "Everything is always working out for me." This is an incredibly grounding perspective to calm and assure yourself when you fear things are going wrong or you're at risk of moving into Force. There is so much you cannot see. You are not the only player in the game, and there are many pieces that need to come together in order create what you most desire. As badly as you want something, as hurried as you feel, it is important to ground yourself in trust, knowing that the timing and course of things are all part of divine alignment.

Do you remember Mark? He would've missed that entire opportunity had he not trusted that intuitive nudge he was offered. A "horrible" experience of being trapped in an elevator was the exact opportunity that allowed him to engage with his new boss. The trusting approach along with that initial reset and realignment led him straight into a "chance" meeting, allowing circumstances to unfold perfectly despite what some might have misinterpreted as a disaster.

- **Listen to your inner voice rather than seeking input and influence from the outside.** Limit the consideration you give other people's opinions and feedback. Know that you are your own best guide and are capable and competent to make choices and act in your best interest. Experiment with your intuition as a muscle you are strengthening regularly. Recognize yourself as skillful and knowledgeable in making decisions, working in conjunction with life, and trusting Flow.

- **Know that you can't get it wrong.** You are always learning, and life is not designed to punish you or make you suffer. You will always get another chance. Every day, every moment is an opportunity to reset and redecide.

❧ SELF-REFLECTION

....

I'm influenced by the energy of other people, places, and things:

☐ SLIGHTLY   ☐ MODERATELY   ☐ TOTALLY

Things that influence my energy in a positive way:

1.

2.

3.

Things that influence my energy in negative ways:

1.

2.

3.

I prefer:

☐ TIME ALONE   ☐ TIME WITH OTHERS   ☐ A MIX OF BOTH

I am comfortable with stillness:

☐ NOT AT ALL   ☐ SOMEWHAT   ☐ COMPLETELY

When I'm still, I experience:

1.

2.

3.

There are times I resist stillness because:

1.

2.

3.

I recognize Flow in the following ways:

1.

2.

3.

I recognize Force in the following ways:

1.

2.

3.

Practices that move me back into Flow include the following:

1.

2.

3.

When I notice the energy of Force, some Reset practices I'm willing to try:

1.

2.

3.

PERSONAL LEARNING:

CHAPTER 5

Environment

*Everything around you, especially your home environment,
mirrors your inner self. So by changing your home, you
also change possibilities in your own life. Removing the
obstacles to the harmonious flow of energy in your living
environment creates more harmony in your life and the
space for wonderful new opportunities to come to you.*

—KAREN KINGSTON

B y now, you've gotten some powerful insight and awareness about
the importance of understanding your inner world and wiring,
along with techniques for maneuvering emotion and energy. Educated,
equipped, and empowered is the name of this game, and now we'll take
this one step further.

ENVIRONMENT—*"the complex of physical, chemical, and biotic factors . . . that act
upon an organism or an ecological community and ultimately
determine its form and survival"*

—MERRIAM-WEBSTER

Environment incorporates everything around you, both seen and
unseen. Whether you're conscious of it or not, its impact on you is
significant. It affects how you feel, your energy, your mental state, and

what you focus on. You've learned that people, places, things, and situations hold energy. In this way, it's essential to assess who and what you're surrounding yourself with, and to understand how they're affecting you. After all, the environment you create and allow for yourself serves as an emotional and energetic home base, one that deserves as much consideration as your internal space.

There is an intensity present in the world that has an urgent, panicked energy to it. Turn on the news, scroll through social media, understand the wording of the thousands of ads you're exposed to, or watch the headlines for even a moment, and you'll feel the weight of it all. Sit in traffic, wait in line, post a political or religious article, and you'll see the intolerance, impatience, and disrespect the people in our world have for one another. Whether you're conscious of it or not, these exposures influence you, and it is critical to assess what you're allowing to exist in your world.

This process begins in your home. Maybe you're unaware of the nuances within your environment, or even if you are aware of them, you're not recognizing the ways they affect you. You might be ignoring or overlooking their impact or have too much leniency for conditions, possessions, and circumstances that aren't serving you well. This tolerance creates the backdrop of your life. Your willingness to live with less-than-acceptable circumstances can indicate a leniency that's counterproductive to your well-being.

With this chapter, you'll look with fresh eyes at the environments where you spend the most time. Your surroundings and the conditions you're operating in will come under the microscope to see how well they're serving you (or not). If your assessment reveals that you're allowing less-than-favorable circumstances, you'll explore ways to clean up and reestablish more ideal surroundings.

WHERE THE HEART IS

Begin with the place you spend most of your time. Your home is your refuge (or at least, that's how it's supposed to feel). It's where you find your connection, rest, and ease. Ideally, the things you surround yourself with promote peace, comfort, and efficiency, and the spaces you've created make you feel happy and grounded. Don't fret if you're finding that is not the case.

Unfortunately, sometimes, we get so wrapped up in our daily lives, in our joys and our stressors, that we fail to notice how the spaces we keep at home may be impacting us on an emotional level. These influences are sometimes easy to spot, but as an Empath, your deep capacity to absorb emotion from your surroundings means that even the subtlest conditions within your home can have a major (and often unseen) impact on your quality of life.

Therefore it's important to take the time to assess how each space within your home makes you feel. Consider carefully the association, feel, and meaning you have with your belongings and the things you allow to take up space in your life. As an Empath, practicing this awareness is every bit as important as assessing your mental, emotional, and energetic well-being.

Consider the following questions:

- If you had to choose one word or phrase to describe your home, what would you use?
- Have you created a space you love?
- Are you surrounded by colors, textures, and smells that serve you well, bring you joy, and reflect your true self?

- What's your motive for keeping things? Are you hanging on to things out of fear and lack or because you feel like you should and are lingering in the past or hoping for that magical "someday"?
- Where do you spend the most time, and how do you feel about being there?

With the answer to that last question in mind, let's narrow the focus to the spaces within your home that matter most. As you do so, realize you're not trying out for the next home improvement show, there's no prize at the end, and no one is calling in the fashion police on you. There's no competition here. No trophies or awards. This is about discovering how you feel on a consistent basis and how your surroundings influence those feelings.

- Living room:
  - What is the feeling you get when you first enter this space?
  - Is your décor updated with things you love to look at?
  - Is your furniture clean and comfortable, or is it torn and tattered, with stains from the kids years ago?
  - Does the space feel good, homey, and comfortable, or does it seem overly cluttered?
  - Do the colors and accessories you surround yourself with bring you joy and help you feel comfortable?
- Kitchen:
  - Are your appliances in working order?
  - Are your counters clean and fairly free of clutter?
  - Are cupboards organized with some sense of functionality and purpose?

- Do you have a place to sit while you eat?
- Do you have the supplies and utensils you need to cook and clean with?
- Is your refrigerator well stocked with foods you enjoy and that make you feel good about yourself?

- Bathroom:
  - Are your shower, sink, and toilet in working order?
  - Are your counters clean and fairly free of clutter?
  - Are cupboards organized with some sense of functionality and purpose?
  - Would you be comfortable letting someone use your bathroom?
  - How fresh or clean are the products you use to care for your body?
  - Do you maintain necessary appointments for teeth cleaning, haircut, checkups, or any of the necessary self-care appointments?

- Bedroom:
  - Is your bed free of clutter? Is their plenty of space to sleep?
  - Do you have the dresser and closet space you need?
  - Are your sheets clean, fitting, and without holes?
  - How do you feel when you go into your closet?
  - Do you use a laundry basket or someplace to put dirty items?
  - Do you put clean laundry away as it is complete?
  - How would you describe your clothes and shoes?
  - Are they comfortable, well fitting, and an accurate reflection of you?

- Office:
  - Do you have the furniture and equipment you need for a productive workday?
  - Can you sit at your desk feeling organized and effective?
  - Are your files and supplies in order?
  - Do you have a place for things you've decided to keep that's organized and easy to find?
  - Do you have a calendar system or way to track notes that doesn't include dozens of sticky notes that easily get lost?
- Vehicle:
  - How safe is your vehicle?
  - How clean is your vehicle?
  - Does driving make you feel stressed or overwhelmed because of the state of your vehicle?
  - Do you use your commute time effectively, listening to something you enjoy, sitting quietly, or talking to someone you love? Or do you fall prey to traffic stressors and tension?
  - When was the last time you scheduled maintenance?

THE CLUTTER WE ALLOW

Imagine trying to go about your day in a room that's pounding with loud music. It's so loud, in fact, that you're unable to hear yourself think. Clutter and mess can create a similar energetic feel. In this way, you can think of clutter as a kind of *visual* noise. The stress and turmoil you're experiencing may be stemming from the chaos in your environment. Untidiness and disorder can be overwhelming and distracting.

Disorganization will create unnecessary difficulties and wreak havoc on how you think and feel.

As an Empath, you may have difficulty channeling and filtering stimuli, and disarray will flood you with distracting minutiae. Your focus is continuously challenged, and your attention seems like a kaleidoscope spread in multiple directions. Cleaning up, eliminating, or adding even small things to your environment will create a more productive, constructive atmosphere.

Consider the story of Donna, a member of one of the coaching groups I conducted years ago. When she surveyed her environment, she discovered several bags of what she referred to as her "cancer clothes." She had been diagnosed with breast cancer and had traveled a long road of treatment and surgeries and was now in a prolonged period of remission. Even so, she held on to the clothes *just in case* the cancer returned.

Wait . . . *what?* Donna was keeping these clothes *just in case* her worst nightmare came true? Even if she didn't actively think about them on a regular basis, she would passively see those bags every single day she walked into her closet to get dressed. In this way, she was allowing those clothes—clothes that represented the very thing she didn't want to happen—to occupy space, energy, and thought within her home.

Donna couldn't see what she was doing until her eyes were opened to this work. After she began an environment assessment, it didn't take her long to realize what she was subconsciously creating and the impact it had on her mindset. Every day, she was submitting subconscious information to her mind, body, and spirit and allowing thoughts and feelings about what she did not want in her life. Unintentionally, she was creating dread for herself every time she opened her closet, and it was her starting point every morning. And because it was her starting point, she spent every day mentally and energetically lingering in that dread, despite eating right, exercising, and changing several habits. All *just in case!*

With the assessment complete, Donna was proud to return to class the next week and share that she had diligently donated every piece of clothing back to the place where she had received it originally. She was ecstatic to keep the generous cycle of giving and receiving by offering those clothes back to the cancer center. And she took joy in being able to use the empty closet space as a new, serene meditation spot. She wrote affirmations on sticky notes to read while she was in there. She cut out positive images of health, decorated with pictures of the beach, and hung family photos to remind her of what she wanted in life.

Donna is a powerful example of environmental energy and assessing motives for keeping and buying specific things. Stuff is far more than just stuff. It holds energy, power, and memory. Everything is energy, and self-awareness and self-honesty allow you to assess your belongings and environment for the things you're accepting in life.

UNDERSTANDING MOTIVES

Actions are visible, though motives are secret.

—SAMUEL JOHNSON

For years, Jerry kept different items around his house that were important to him, mostly items representing the past. Even as he neared an age when it becomes vital to assess belongings for the sake of those left behind, Jerry remained obstinate about the things he clung to. His grown children were becoming more vocal about the state of his home, and what started off as helpful suggestions came to a head when he found his youngest son sneaking some of his belongings out to the garbage. The confrontation was not a pretty one.

Things grew worse when his other children and their spouses got involved, resulting in a very harsh exchange and even sharper threats. The family persisted, and eventually everyone erupted in rage, leaving Jerry defeated and deflated in a pile of tears. The kids were shocked, as they had never seen their father shed a tear, even in the face of family tragedy.

The conversation finally resulted in Jerry's emotional unraveling of layers of pain he kept hidden under those piles of old stuff. The things others saw as garbage, waste, and clutter were emotionally tied tightly to his greatest memories and deepest pain.

Jerry and his wife were married for forty-nine years, and they had been together since he was sixteen. She died six days before their fiftieth wedding anniversary, and every day felt like a struggle to breathe without her. Her toothbrush still hung in their bathroom, and her clothes were still neatly folded in her dresser drawers, just as she had left them.

Equally painful was what others referred to as the "spare room," but what Jerry still called "Peter's room." Peter was their middle son who died tragically when he was only eight, and though his items had all been cleared from the closest and the drawers, the room was still decorated with Peter's memorabilia.

This dilapidated home was filled with stuff that most would neither recognize nor appreciate. Yet, to Jerry, it was the floodwall of pain he used to keep things tightly sealed, maintaining his suppression and denial of hard times, allowing him to pretend that his beloved family members were just away for a while or out to the store. The act of tugging at Jerry's possessions unraveled those layered defenses that hid years of agonizing pain. Once they understood the trauma and turmoil Jerry still held, the family was able to take a more delicate approach to helping clean up his home.

Jerry's story reflects an important point to consider when you're assessing your environment and the things you choose to keep: *what* you're doing is the physical display of your inner working; *why* you're doing it is not visible, nor easily understood. Determining the *why* that drives your behavior is a critical component of this work. Motives can be obscure, multifaceted, and subconscious, requiring some investigation and self-honesty. Sometimes there's not just one reason why you're doing something. It's common to have multiple reasons, and it's important to tease them apart to see them clearly.

Motives are the *why* of your decisions that create an energetic under-current, promoting a certain feel that will attract specific results. Your motives determine your approach, outlook, and mood, even subconsciously. Doing something nice for someone because you want them to like you may seem kind, but it's self-serving. Making sales calls from a place of fear, lack, or competition has scarcity woven into the fabric of how you show up and a sense people get from you. It taints your perspective and results. Motives may be energetic and subliminal, but people can certainly sense and detect them.

No one has pure motives 100 percent of the time. A lot of what we do is intended to serve some purpose or function for ourselves. It's normal. Wanting to look good, win at something, be included, land the account, get a date, or trying to gain favor may all be normal motives when sprinkled in with other clearer, healthier motives, such as contribution, service, and alignment with life purpose. Be honest with yourself in addressing your main drive.

It is important to understand the mindset and approach you take to life. Have you ever met someone who is highly anxious, tries too hard, or stumbles over themselves with angst and awkwardness? How about someone who is doubting and suspicious of others? Or someone who is hostile and defensive about things? This energy reflects their inner workings and outlook, which sets the tone and creates a lens of how they approach life and decisions.

What's the undercurrent pulsing through your perspective and the things you create and allow? Are you fearful that you'll never get what you want? Do you worry that others will get ahead, and believe you need to work hard to prove yourself to get what's coming to you? Are you anxious and overly concerned about what others think? Are you lost in competition with others? Does doubt and worry keep you from enjoying yourself and trusting the process? Do you fall prey to those patterns of perfecting, performing, and pleasing, always trying to gain approval and acceptance from others?

Be diligent about what you're exposing yourself to and the mindset you've established, especially first thing in the morning. Recognize the influence certain things have on your emotion and energy levels. Carefully decipher the motives you're driven from, the tone or undercurrent they create, and the impact it all has.

DO YOU LOVE IT?

After Beth and I stopped to get lunch, we decided to check out a cute shop that recently opened around the corner. It was a great afternoon full of free-flowing conversation and laughter—at least until we stepped into the checkout lane. She looked at the item in my hands and simply asked, "Do you love it?" Such an innocent question left me pondering, *Do I? Do I really love this item I'm about to spend money on and bring into my home?*

I was slightly saddened when the resounding internal voice spoke a solid no. What I liked was the price, the fun of buying something and spending time with my friend, and the joyful energy of the day. The item itself was cute, but I certainly did not love it. So, I returned it to its home on the shelf.

From that day forward, I incorporated that question, "Do I love it?" as a guideline for buying. If the answer is a solid yes, I allow myself to purchase the item. If it is any other answer or motive, I commit to leaving it in the store. I must admit, it's sometimes still a challenge to avoid buying something I don't fully love, but it gets easier with time and has even become quite motivating for other areas in life.

As you assess your motives for buying and keeping things, you can check for the unhealthy energy you're allowing in your environment. Keeping something out of fear or obligation has a very different feel to it than joy and pleasure. Having gobs of stuff piled on shelves, or keeping crammed closets, is quite different from having special items beautifully displayed where you can see and enjoy them as you wish. Buying in excess promotes an undercurrent of fear and distrust that your needs will not be met. It alters your perspective about things. On the other hand, establishing a firm foundation of faith and trust allows healthy motives to determine what you're doing and why you're doing it. This in turn offers confidence and assurance to an anxious mind.

Challenge yourself and dig deep to recognize what you're doing and why. Determine the energy that fuels your decisions. Develop clear standards for keeping and purchasing things. Commit to helpful criteria such as having a need, enjoyment, satisfaction, or the prospect for growth and learning before you even entertain the possibility of bringing something into your environment and your life. Allow only items that are functional and that you love, and those things will contribute to a deliberate energy and expectation within your environment. There's no settling, *good enough* tolerance here. With this discipline driving your decisions, you will recognize your patterns more clearly, bringing to light any unhelpful habits, items, or behaviors that aren't serving you.

INNER AND OUTER

Years ago, I heard it said, "As is the outer, so is the inner." This offered a necessary observation that what's happening in your outer world is the result of what's occurring in your inner environment. Because these two are inextricably linked, the reverse is also true. Consistent practices that challenge you to clean up, organize, declutter, and rearrange will shake up your physical, mental, emotional, and spiritual energy and habits.

Your environment will either support or deplete you. Holding on to things with motives of fear, habit, obligation, or lack, creates blind spots or a tendency to overlook or ignore the toll these take. You are committing to fear and lack rather than abundance and possibilities. Develop awareness and discipline regarding not only the things you purchase, but also establish "keeping standards." Keep only those things that enhance your life, improve ease and effectiveness, and bring you joy, trusting that you will always have what you need.

Commit to buying and keeping things you love, that you truly need, and that make your life easier and happier. See how it feels and how it impacts you. Not only will your budget be lighter, but so will your energy. The time you save not shopping, scrolling, cleaning, searching for things, or sorting will be significant. Using that time, energy, effort, and money differently will add meaning and purpose to your life if you're intentional about using them differently.

Remember, everything is energy. Your possessions hold significant history and emotion. Changing habits and ridding your environment can really stir up that emotion. Having the awareness and courage to face this work is an incredible step. Creating space that allows for ease, calm, and effectiveness in your mind, spirit, and heart can be life changing, and it may take some time to adjust. You don't have to do this alone. It may be easier to work through this with the assistance and accountability of someone who is healthy and supportive.

Be mindful of every place you put your hands, feet, and eyes as you assess your spaces with a fresh perspective. This includes areas such as your bedroom, main living area, bathroom, desk, car, office, closet, etc. This is your opportunity to consider what you're allowing to occupy your space and evaluate their impact.

Environment is everything around you, so take this as far as you would like and into as many areas as you prefer. For instance, once you are done with your physical environment, you might explore your social media feed, email inbox, finances, subscriptions, etc. This is yours to do as much or as little with as you're ready. Again, we're not out to win any awards. There are no Enlightenment police monitoring this. It's simply a matter of your readiness and willingness to take on another layer of this work to empower you and support you in this empathic journey.

❧ ENVIRONMENT ASSESSMENT

A word or phrase I would use to describe my environment:

The feeling I get when I think about my environment:

My motives for buying often include the following:

1.
2.
3.

I allow sales or coupons to motivate me to buy things I don't want or need.

☐ RARELY ☐ SOMETIMES ☐ OFTEN

I buy things I don't need out of fear or a scarcity mentality.

☐ RARELY ☐ SOMETIMES ☐ OFTEN

I keep things "just in case," or in the hope that I'll use it someday.

☐ RARELY ☐ SOMETIMES ☐ OFTEN

I hold on to things out of habit, sentiment, or obligation.

☐ RARELY ☐ SOMETIMES ☐ OFTEN

There's a sense of clutter or mess in my home:

☐ NOT AT ALL   ☐ SOMEWHAT   ☐ COMPLETELY

If I only kept the things I love and that are in working order, I would eliminate the following:

1.
2.
3.
4.
5.

Ultimately, I want to create an environment that:

Things that need my attention:

1.
2.
3.
4.
5.

Things I'm ready to take action on:

1.
2.
3.
4.
5.

CHAPTER 6

The Equipped Empath

There's nobody who cares more about you than you, and there's nobody better equipped to take care of you than you.

—RUSH LIMBAUGH

EQUIP—*"to supply with the necessary items for a particular purpose"*
"prepare mentally for a particular situation or task"

—OXFORD LANGUAGES

RESOURCE—*"a source of supply or support"*
"a natural feature or phenomenon that enhances the quality of life"
"a possibility of relief or recovery"
" an ability to meet or handle a situation"

—MERRIAM-WEBSTER

Janay sat several states away, but even with all that distance between us, I could feel her angst and overwhelm through the computer screen. She had been waffling about a hefty life decision, caught in the loop of possibilities, and feeling paralyzed about what to do. She was overthinking, doubtful, seeking others' opinions, and worried about the options she *didn't* choose. Finally, she threw up her hands and said, "Where's the real adult who knows how to decide this stuff?"

Have you looked around and secretly wondered, "Well, who's going to handle this mess?" and felt jolted by the horrifying realization that life is up to you? Simply deciding what to make for dinner can seem overwhelming, to say nothing of trying to make a career move, where to live, who to date, whether to marry, have a child, or any major life option. Being an adult can be hard, and that dreaded imposter syndrome may have you faking it most days.

Equipped, competent, capable, prepared, qualified, resourceful . . . would these be words you would use to describe yourself? As an Empath who can feel saturated, overloaded, bothered, burdened, overwhelmed, and encumbered by life, *equipped* might not be something that sounds possible for you. Up to now, you may never have felt prepared for what life threw at you, whether it was big or small.

Have you stopped to consider the tools, resources, and methods you use to get through life? Who taught you how to deal, cope, problem solve, or manage conflict? What was role modeled for you? When a problem hits, a hard conversation needs to be had, or a challenging decision needs to be made, what do you do? What resources do you draw upon?

The good news is that, as an Empath who's conscious and aware of the feelings and needs of others, you've probably figured out a wide range of tools and resources for navigating situations and dealing with people. The bad news, however, is that some of your coping mechanisms might not be very healthy or effective. Since you experience life in ways that others don't, you may struggle more deeply with making decisions and feeling capable of processing information and options.

Not to worry! With this chapter, we're going to focus on ways to strengthen and fortify you—mind, body, and spirit. You'll learn to incorporate tools, resources, and practices to utilize and align with your mind, body, emotions, and spirit. Feeling capable and qualified with a well-stocked toolbox will propel you into an empowered stance. Because after all, a properly equipped Empath is an Enlightened Empath!

DEEP WATERS

Suzy was my best friend in second grade, so I was taken aback when she announced one morning that she and her family were moving away. We'd been friends since kindergarten. She'd come to all my birthday parties and had stayed over many nights for fun childhood adventures. At such an early age, I couldn't comprehend what moving away entailed, but I could feel from my friend that it was not a good thing. Suzy was sad and disheartened the last few days of school, and I could feel her pain and assume her interpretation of the experience. On her last day, I cried so hard at my desk that my teacher sent me to the corner for disrupting class. The other students taunted me for being a crybaby.

Emotions can feel big and heavy for Empaths—like treading through deep waters. The emotions and experiences of those around you may seem as though they are your own, and you may struggle to distinguish what's yours versus what belongs to other people. Further, if your intuition has been shut down, shamed, or made fun of, it's hard to fully understand the really big emotions, whether those emotions are yours or they belong to someone else. Experiences such as these are hard to recover from when there's no support or understanding, and even worse if you're told you're the problem, wrong, crazy, or overreacting. The work in this chapter will help you navigate those deep waters.

The divine power of intuition allows you to recover from those old messages and experiences. As you move fully into your body with Embodiment work and listen to the wisdom of intuition, you'll be strengthened and empowered. You can move away from the limitations of logic, habit, obligation, and expectation and more fully into your body. Those old stories that something is wrong with you will fall away as you step into a new understanding, respect, and appreciation for what you're experiencing.

THE GIFT OF INTUITION

Enlightenment empowers you with a greater level of knowledge, functioning, and relating. Having dealt with the previous chapters and topics, you're now conscious of many different tools, techniques, and areas of focus. Have you made friends with your internal GPS (Gut, Perception, and Senses)? Learning to do this is a powerful start! Developing an intimate, trusting relationship with your intuition is an essential step in becoming equipped.

Intuition is defined by Oxford Languages as "the ability to understand something immediately, without the need for conscious reasoning" and "a thing that one knows or considers likely from instinctive feeling rather than conscious reasoning."

Intuition is also known as instinct, a nudge, an inkling, your gut, hunch, knowing, feeling, or a sense. It doesn't matter what you call it; it just matters that you familiarize yourself with it and the ways it coaxes and communicates with you. Like a coach who simply wants you to win the game, intuition is on your side and is a valuable guide for navigating life. Practice doesn't really make perfect, but it does increase your ability to recognize your intuition and align with its powerful nudges. Tuning in to and trusting your insight is like building muscle for a healthier lifestyle. It's a steadfast practice that requires consistency and deliberate focus.

Lana shared about the one time she remembers being spanked as a child. "Of all the naughty things I did when I was little, it's the strangest thing that I was only ever punished for crying in church." She paused to reflect for a moment before asking rhetorically, "Can you imagine?

I could *feel* the prayers, music, and people around me. I didn't understand what was happening, and they told me to stop, but the tears would flood out of me. When I got home, I got spanked . . . crazy." Her voice trailed off, and it took her a few minutes to come back from that memory.

What we learn from this story is that an adult's confused interpretation of energy and emotion can distort a child's intuition, sensory experience, and perception. Lana's experience was completely misunderstood, leading her to believe she was misbehaving and to feel ashamed and anxious about those parts of her that could perceive and pick up on energy.

Before life begins to distract and dissuade them, kids are highly in touch with this sense of knowing—like little Danny, who won't go near odd Uncle Fred and cries every time he's told he's rude for not wanting to; or like Sandra, who innocently breaks into dance at the first beat of a tune and twirls aimlessly in the middle of the store, not worrying about how she looks or what people might think of her but is told to "knock it off." Or like Andy, who begins to tense and cry when his parents are stressed and angry over a financial conversation at the dinner table, and he's told to stop being a girl and mind his own business. Kids instinctively sense and detect things, and the ways that is explained and handled by adults significantly impacts them.

The gut knows and can sense things you might not be able to verbalize or understand, and as an Empath, you can detect things that others can't. Somewhere along the way, you have been talked out of, shamed, ridiculed, made fun of, and even punished for the ways you've handled and interpreted your emotion and sensory insights. The Empath's Toolbox will draw you to that powerful insight, instinct, and knowing of Enlightenment.

WHERE THE ROAD MAY LEAD

As a wise and watchful friend, intuition deserves your trust and respect. Familiarize yourself with the ways it speaks to you, including the gentle nudges, whispers, pokes, and prods. It knows things that logic will dismiss, fear will caution against, and others will doubt. Intuition is a divine communicator that knows what's in your best interest and highest opportunity. The biblical story of Noah reflects this deep knowing that should be trusted despite logic, reason, current circumstances, or the opinions of others.

The key to overriding the voices of outside influencers is to learn to trust your intuition by moving from your head into your body. This is a matter of commitment as you learn the feel and steadfastness of intuition. Take a breath, lighten up, and have some fun as you allow yourself to practice and experiment with your hunches. Declare a specific period (an hour, a week) that you will use to explore and honor what your gut is telling you. Commit to listening to it and be willing to play out whatever the gut is directing you to do.

As with a new partner you're not sure you can trust yet and haven't quite established ease and familiarity with, it will take some time and several tried and true experiences to become acquainted with the intuition, to trust its reliability, consistency, and availability. Just as you work over time to establish a firm, safe foundation with a beloved partner, so too can you get to know and familiarize yourself with the nuances, quirks, and set ways of the intuition. Learning these is a process and requires your willingness to try those trust falls and test the safety and solidarity of your intuition. Knowing that safe arms catch you each time helps establish that reliance and submission.

Instinct has a distinct feel with subtlety and steadfastness to it.

Instinct and intuition speak clearly and calmly. These nudges are not chaotic, destructive, or frantic. They won't cause harm, misdirect, or do damage. They are intended to direct, protect, and guide as you learn to lean into their safety, trust, and familiarity.

Start with small steps. Take a different route home, try a new food, or drink that stands out on the menu, send an email to inquire about something you want to learn more about, call someone you thought of recently. Stay out of your head as much as possible. Don't overthink, lock in on outcomes, or predetermine timelines, as these tendencies will pinch off your intuition. Stay open and see what happens.

One of my favorite ways to work on this is through a fun practice I refer to as "Turn Right Here Adventures." My friends and family know this is something I started to play with years ago, and though it often makes no sense to them, they know by now that the miracles that have unfolded from these experiments have been astounding. As I'm driving (or someone else who's courageous enough to play along is driving) I tune in and inquire where I'm meant to go. Every once in a while, I'll receive a subtle nudge from my intuition. I've learned to honor these, even if it means moving off my preferred, predetermined course. When I have an impulse that speaks to me, I start to feel a funny, curious sensation in my gut, and I know I'm meant to make a turn ahead. The magic is about to begin.

Recently, while vacationing in Florida, I was excited to head to the beach when I received a nudge from my intuition to turn away from my intended route. A year prior, I probably would have laughed off the feeling as ridiculous. I mean, it still seems slightly criminal to postpone a day of sunshine and fun even for a few moments. But by the time of my vacation, I knew enough to follow the nudge. After all, the beach would still be waiting once my intuition nudged me back to it.

So, I followed my intuition to a new road, uncertain but excited about what might take place. I remember feeling a bit impatient as the road continued to unfold, but before long, I got another nudge to turn left again. Just as I did, a field off to the left revealed itself. I parked the car and walked into the field, only to encounter a distant swarm of four-legged creatures so low to the ground I could barely make them out. As I waded deeper into that random grassland, I was finally able to depict a sea of turtles, perhaps ten or twelve of them, just hanging out doing their turtle thing in the warm sunshine. It was majestic and breathtaking.

I know it sounds crazy. It sounds crazy even to me, and I was there. I was *called* off the beaten path, led miles down a country road to a random field filled with one of my favorite animals. For what seemed like hours, I sat at the edge of the field watching my new turtle friends. They moseyed by, and if I didn't get too close, they allowed me to sit among them. Tears filled my eyes and emotion welled up at the magic I was observing. There were just so many of them! Laughter erupted when I thought, *Who's going to believe that I found a field of magic just because a little voice inside told me to?* It didn't matter, because I saw it and felt it and knew it was yet one more intuitive gift that had been offered.

Later that evening I googled "turtle animal spirit guide," and information deepened the impact of the turtle adventure. The meaning included messages about slowing down, setting pace, and staying grounded. Continued searching furthered the confirmation to stay true to my path, creating a sense of home wherever I may be, and finally, the need to reconnect to Mother Earth. Incredible!

Recently, my friend Samantha and I were on an adventure together through the hills of Kentucky, and I was thankful to be behind the wheel because she hadn't quite bought into my "Turn Right Here" mentality.

The farther the winding roads led us into those country hollers, the more uncomfortable Sam became. Over and over again, she insisted that she heard banjos playing in the hills. Yet, I *knew* something was calling us.

The road continued to wind, and just as I was beginning to waiver, I saw it. On the smallest roadside marker, I spotted a sign assuring me that we were on the right path. And so, we continued along, only to discover the quaintest pottery shop I've ever seen. I felt the magic before we even turned into the parking lot.

We spent an afternoon with the woman and her son, who ran the business together. They gave us a tour, showed us their pieces, offered us coffee, allowed us to hold and pet their animals, and even let us take a spin at the pottery wheel to see how it all worked. It was a day I'll never forget—a day so remarkable that even Samantha wound up putting more stock in these "Turn Right Here" experiences.

I could write about dozens of these experiences, times I've been led in a direction I didn't understand or necessarily agree with. Some have taken me to waterfalls or to cliffs to hike; others to meet some of the coolest people I never would've known; still others to quaint roadside shops with hidden treasures and local people with amazing tales to share. Some have led me to parks where I've collected majestic rocks or sat under trees filled with generations of strength and wisdom. Some have left me wandering down an empty road where I soon realized there was nothing to see along the way. Whenever that has happened, I have chosen to believe that there was something on that other road I was meant to be detoured from. There are no words to describe the magic of experiences like these, nor the divine humility I feel about being guided into the most breathtaking moments of my life.

These nudges aren't reserved for "Turn Right Here" adventures. There's a strong parallel to the greater scope in which life is constantly pointing and directing you in every area. These experiences are fun and have fairy-tale magic to them, and they offer powerful insight to the all-encompassing, divine protection and guidance you're offered throughout life. Stay open, curious, and willing to listen, trust, and follow through.

Give it a whirl. Take a field trip with your inner GPS, literally or figuratively. Allow yourself the freedom of no agenda, time frame, outcome, or plan, just an openness to discover where your intuition is directing you. Keep an open mind to see where you're being guided. Then, grab a notebook and start documenting your experiences.

TO THINE OWN SELF BE TRUE

Like a new friend you enjoy being with, make the time and space to get to know this magnificent part of you called your *intuition*. You have a personal responsibility to do what it takes to be at your best physically, emotionally, and spiritually. Establish yourself as a priority. It's not selfish; it's essential. These instinctual nudges are leading you in a direction even if you don't understand or like it. Trust the process and see what happens as you experiment and play with the ways it speaks to you.

Awareness, self-care, and accountability are vital in this process to decipher what is self-will versus the will of your intuition. They feel differently, and the more you practice, the more familiar you'll become with intuition's Divine Guidance. This process is intended to keep you in the driver's seat of your life, allowing you to navigate circumstances, decisions, and relationships from an empowered position as you're intuitively led.

As your own best guide and the expert of your life, you may need to assess or even break up with those negative voices in your head and demote the people you've allowed to weigh in on your decisions. Managing your commodities of time, energy, and effort along with setting boundaries and clarifying your needs and preferences will allow you to be emotionally and energetically "clutter-free," providing room and permission for the intuition to clearly communicate with you.

WHERE'S YOUR FOCUS?

Imagine life as a spectacular buffet. There's so much readily available to you in quantities beyond measure, but as you grab your plate and fork, you find yourself focusing solely on the items that aren't appealing to you. You pick and prod at the foods you don't actually want, concentrating on the colors and textures that aren't pleasing. You initiate conversation with other guests, inquire with the servers, and finally summon the manager to complain about the foods you don't like. As the kind manager encourages you to partake in all the alternatives that are available, you immediately go back to the complaint department of life, honing your disdain for those displeasing options. You put your plate down and stew in the misery of the experience, feeling sullen and swollen as you watch everyone else enjoy their meals.

Absurd, isn't it? An impressive array available at your fingertips but your focus is steadfast on what you don't want, causing you to miss a grand opportunity to embrace and enjoy everything you do want. The energy that goes into this focus of complaining is damaging for a number of reasons, but primarily because it establishes your focus and equally draws other people into it while solidifying your perspective into a negative space.

When something happens, how do you approach or interpret it? What is your gut reaction? Do you immediately slip into fear and resistance? Do you seek input, validation, and suggestions from others, or do you tune in, get quiet, and seek spiritual guidance? What's your perspective when life gets hard, your feelings get hurt, or people don't do what they said they were going to do? Are you focused on the wrongs of the world and ruminate that things aren't the way you want them to be? Have you set up camp at the complaint department, focusing your mind, thoughts, and conversations around how bad things are? Do you look around in comparison, judgment, and jealousy of others?

Where you look is where you go, and if you are concentrating on the wrongs of life, those wrongs become the center of your attention. This is risky because it limits your focus and prevents you from seeing options, possibilities, and opportunities. As you learn to use the powerful tool of your GPS, it is important to center your attention on the things you *do* want. Steer clear of thoughts and conversations that concentrate on what you don't want or what isn't working. Frame your vision and your language into a positive context so you can be narrowly focused on the good you want to attract.

Take a moment to get still, take a deep breath, and think of the word *giggle*. Feel what happens inside your body. What images come to mind? What are your thoughts, and how do they influence your energy? Now take a minute to really feel into that word and close your eyes. Try that again and again with different words to recognize the way one simple word can shift and lighten your mood and perspective.

Now, I'd like you to feel the contrast. Take another breath. Consider the word *hate*. Take it in for only a moment but notice where that word lands in your body. Can you feel the difference? Words matter. Thoughts matter. They are a foundational step in equipping your properly.

178

Emotional and energetic practices are critical for centering your mind, body, and spirit with crystal clear focus on what you want. Proactive measures, deliberate practices, and selective thoughts, words, and focus keep you aware and alert by managing your emotions, environment, energy, and engagements, consistently positioning you in alignment with intuition and Flow and launching into Enlightenment.

BE STILL AND KNOW

What's your take on solitude? It's an interesting concept that deserves your attention. Have you ever been somewhere and someone asked, "Are you by yourself?" as though it were a bad thing? Or seen someone out eating or walking alone and you start to assume a tragic, lonely story? Our society does weird things with aloneness, assigns false meaning to it, and is presumptuous when someone is flying solo, as though it's the worst possible company you could have.

As an Empath, solitude, stillness, and reflection are necessary to allow you the time and space to check in with yourself. Solitude, for a few moments or an extended season, can offer you profound insight and opportunity to know and embrace yourself and your giftedness. Establishing consistent practices and utilizing various methods allows you to reestablish deep, meaningful connection with your very best self.

Does the sheer thought of solitude send you into a panic? How do you handle alone time, and what meaning do you assign to it? Are you embarrassed, ashamed, or feel unworthy when you aren't surrounded by people or things to do? Do you have faulty beliefs about being alone and what that means about you? Do you use busyness or perceived obligations to other people as a way to cope or distract yourself?

Or, you may have a very different perspective about this idea of solitude. Do you long for it at every turn? Do privacy and seclusion afford you the peace and ease you need that you can't find among a crowd? Is "peopling" much harder for you, and solitude is your refuge? Are social interactions uncomfortable enough that you tend to avoid them? Do you isolate and avoid interaction altogether?

Solitude is another concept that's important to dissect in order to understand your beliefs and assumptions about what it means to you. Even if it makes you uncomfortable at first, solitude is a powerful way to reset, recharge, and eliminate the outside voices and energy. This clears the clutter, noise, and distraction, providing the opportunity for you to familiarize yourself with your own voice, feelings, needs, and desires—all of which are contributing components of intuition that help you tune in to and follow your GPS.

You have a personal responsibility to decide what feels right to you. It's likely to change from day to day, and you may have different seasons of needing more solitude versus more socialization. No one else is responsible for dictating or deciding how you should or shouldn't engage. Also, others can't read your mind. Your need for solitude is yours to get comfortable with, communicate, and assert.

Keep in mind there's a difference between insulation and isolation. Insulation is a safe, protected feeling that allows you to unwind, dissimulate, debrief, and reregulate. If you find comfort, rest, and refuge by insulating in your home or being by yourself, then take full advantage of those opportunities when they come. If, however, you favor *isolation*—where you're unable to go out or socialize at all—then learning strategies to manage necessary interactions will be beneficial and relieving to you.

It is important to recognize the balance. A daily practice of introspection and quiet is both hygienic and nourishing to the soul. Two minutes, twenty minutes, or two hours of reflection will serve you well. It's a mini check-in to assess and regulate. You get to decide what your practice looks like. It can be guided meditation, prayer, breath work, sitting quietly, walking meditation, writing, chanting, anything you choose. There are no right or wrong ways to do this. The goal is simple: to tune inward and align more with your intuition.

I have several daily practices of tuning inward, cleansing energy, and spiritual alignment that have become easy, fun, and practical. My morning routine incorporates a dimly lit shower in which I sing, pray, chant, and reflect. I incorporate deep-breath work and intentional reflection of gratitude and praise. As I'm drying my hair, I do mirror reflections in which I run through a long list of "I am" affirmations. I'm already standing in front of the mirror looking at myself; might as well make good use of it.

When I'm in the office seeing clients, like clockwork, just before every hour, I make the small trek down the hall to the restroom. My steps are intentional as I release the energy and emotion from the past session and prepare to move into the next. Aside from the obvious bathroom business, I again use the water and soap to ground myself through the feel and the smell of the experience. And just like the morning routine, I utilize the mirror to do a few more grounding, releasing affirmations, and I'm reset and renewed for the next experience.

Your routines can be simple and easily incorporated into things you're already doing. The point is to check in, move energy, and reconnect with yourself and a Higher Source to keep you in tune, regulated, and attentive to what's happening. No one needs to know; it doesn't have to be a production. You don't need to spend hours or climb to a mountaintop to connect with yourself. Allow it to be easy, fun, and essential.

Carving a consistent space for quiet, stillness, and reflection will offer you endless possibilities to tap into a deeper spiritual sense.

Practice the Noticing Breath without judgment or evaluation to observe and witness your internal chatter, energy, and environment both internally and externally. Every time your "monkey mind" runs amuck, bouncing from mental limb to mental limb, you simply notice it and bring it back to a word, mantra, or breath, allowing yourself to center and ground.

Meditation will be a lifeline as you learn to tune in and align with your body and spirit. The good news is you can't do it wrong! You can't screw up an attempt at meditation or mindfulness. You don't need to find yourself in perfect posture and at unflinching inner peace like a long-practiced guru. No matter what meditation looks like for you, any period of stillness, quiet, and turning inward is a successful attempt.

These practices enable you to approach life feeling prepared and capable, which will launch you to new levels of strength, clarity, and assurance. It is then that you can begin to equip yourself with the tools, tips, and techniques that can benefit an Empath in managing energy, decision-making, navigating relationships, and dealing with conflict.

Like different tools in a toolbox, take your time to familiarize and practice each of the techniques that follow. They will enable you to use your body, breath, and brain in conjunction with your intuition. Meditation is a foundational step. Once you've learned to check in, quiet your mind, and listen to your intuition, knowing which tool is right for the job will equip you in profound ways.

THE EMPATH'S TOOLBOX

What follows is a series of techniques to add to your toolbox. If you can develop a consistent practice of these techniques, then you will find yourself firmly rooted, embodied, and in tune with your intuition. A morning routine with any of these practices has a way of launching you into the day, but it does not have to happen in the morning. Practice using them anytime, especially when you are feeling stressed, depleted, or are experiencing a lot of energy.

Protection

PROTECT—*"to cover or shield from exposure, injury, damage, or destruction"*
"defend"

—MERRIAM-WEBSTER

For an Empath, "protection" is a noteworthy kind of energy that allows you to defend yourself from other energies that might put you into a negative space. Protection is necessary at times, but because it is such a closed and guarded stance, I recommend you use it selectively and with intention.

If you have difficulty being in the world or engaging with people, you may believe that protection is always necessary, an instinct that causes you to take defensive measures that have helped you get by, or even survive. You may suit up to protect yourself when you go into the world, so you're not impacted by outside influences. The caution is that this "suiting up" can be like wearing heavy armor that isn't required for everyday use. When you use this armor too often, it can shape your perception and assumptions about people and their intentions. In other words, that heavy defense becomes unnecessary baggage.

Further, if you consistently use protection as a coping strategy, it will become the lens through which you see things. Your mind will be tuned to perceive threats and a lack of safety. The resulting energy will create an assumption that there's something to defend against, even when there isn't. It can cause you to go through life with your dukes up, guarded,

183

ready to fight and shield, leaving no room for your trusted intuition to do what it needs to do to guide and direct you.

All that said, protection is one of the most important tools in your toolbox. You simply need to learn when and where to use it. When you're interacting with unsafe, unkind people or dealing with stressful, precarious circumstances, I encourage you to shore up and protect yourself with some necessary grounding and safeguarding. Just remember that it is easy to fall back into protection mode, and falling back too often can isolate you in unproductive, unnecessary ways.

As you become more enlightened, you begin to use protective measures only when they are necessary. You become increasingly equipped and capable of managing stressors, conflict, or difficulties as they arise. You'll use protective techniques mindfully and intentionally, knowing that they can block out as much good energy as negative or questionable energy. The more you do this work, the more you'll trust yourself to effectively use this important tool.

Consider the following exercises to help you master the tool of protection:

- Visualization—A shelter of white light, an aura, a shield, or a cloak can be powerful images that allow a layer of protection when you're in the company of others. Use these images to surround you to keep their energy out of your field or to envelop other people to allow them to keep and manage their own energy.
- Imagine a wall of mirrors to reflect others' energy back to them.
- Use a power word that strengthens and focuses you to deflect emotions, words, or energy that doesn't belong to you.
- Wear a crystal or medallion around your neck to protect your heart center.

- Imagine a circle of white light or a blanket of love and safety to wrap others in.
- Place your hand on your heart center to guard energy absorption.
- Envision an energetic Hula-Hoop around you. Think of this as a defined, distinct area that separates you from others. You stay inside of it and others stay out. You can shrink or expand the size of your Hula-Hoop at any point based on your feelings and needs.

Detachment

DETACH—*"to separate, especially from a larger mass and usually without violence"*

—MERRIAM-WEBSTER

The practice of detachment creates space and separation from others emotionally, energetically, or physically without the defensive energy of protection.

- Imagine white light encompassing others so their experience remains their own. This allows you to be present without absorbing their energy.
- Visualize cutting chords that have connected you to others.
- Imagine a *Return to Sender* stamp that you can use to send someone's energy back to them.
- Remain conscious and aware of how people, places, and things impact you so you can establish proper boundaries.
- Be mindful of your language. If you take on others' emotions and experience, allow separation even in your language. Don't couple yourself into their emotion with words such as *we* (e.g.,

"How are we feeling today?" "What are we going to do about that?"). Establish distinct separation with your words and body language (e.g., "How are you feeling today?" "What do you need to do about that?")

Cleansing

Emotion and energy can feel heavy, thick, dirty, or polluted. If you recognize that your energy is low or you are feeling clogged or contaminated, then cleansing is in order. This technique allows you to purify and purge anything that's not serving you. Just as you've practiced maintaining your mood, thoughts, beliefs, and environment, so it is with your energy. Self-awareness allows you immediate access to what feels good and what doesn't so you can be mindful when you need to cleanse.

- Do not underestimate the healing and cleansing powers of an Epsom salt bath. Add some essential oils and candles to make it even more effective.
- Perform breath work to move and purify your energy and thoughts. Breathe it out deeply and heavily or smoothly and consistently.
- Incorporate calming scents with essential oils, candles, or incense in places you spend the most time.
- Use sage to energetically cleanse yourself, others, or a space.
- Write it down and then burn what you've written to rid yourself of the unwanted energy.
- Engage with movement that makes you feel as if you are cleansing yourself. Jump up and down, stomp, sprint, or use any method that allows you to dispel energy. Sweep yourself off with your hands after a difficult interaction.

- Be in and around water as much as possible. Be mindful and fully present in the shower or bath to allow yourself to experience the cleansing effects of water. Incorporate water in your home and in your routine wherever possible. Visit water as often as you can (creeks, lakes, ponds, oceans, and even puddles can be a lot of fun). Also, make sure you are drinking plenty of water.
- Imagine love or pure white light sweeping through your body to replace dark energy.
- Find a Reiki practitioner.
- Find a Qigong routine you like.

Grounding

As an Empath who collects and absorbs emotion and energy from all kinds of sources, it is essential to release anything that isn't yours or isn't serving you. Grounding is a way to stay fully present in your body and be firmly planted and rooted and in the best position to release the energy you don't need. When you feel stressed, distracted, or erratic, grounding allows you to establish your focus and your footing.

- Put your palms firmly against your opposite arm and repeat, "I am here now." See your feet on the ground and center your mind on the present moment.
- Feel your feet on the earth, your back against the chair, or your butt in the seat to get yourself centered and present. Feel the security of being held when you are sitting or lying down. Rub your feet on the floor and feel the support and power of the earth.
- Integrate each of your senses to calm, regulate, or stimulate yourself. Touch, smell, see, taste, and listen to what's around

you to acclimate to your environment. Identify three things you see; touch a few things with different textures to notice varying sensations; take a whiff of something in the room even as odd as that may seem. Sensory experiences have profound effects on your ability to be present and centered.

- Be mindful of your stance and the energy it promotes and conveys. Place your feet firmly on the ground. Square your shoulders and keep your head up. You certainly don't need to be rigid or extreme, but posture, stance, and position send messages and convey energy. Be mindful of what you're communicating. A stance with the head up, heart forward, and shoulders squared can be very empowering.

- Call your energy back to yourself after challenging engagements. Feel it fill your body.

- Implement the Power Pose. It's energizing and will launch you into the next level of confidence. Stand firmly planted on the ground with your hands on your hips and head held high as you visualize whatever it is you're about to experience. Breathe deep into your body and feel the power.

- Raise up on your tiptoes and pound your heels to the ground, like how you might pound a bag of flour on the counter to settle it.

- Picture roots or cords of light coming out of your feet and traveling deep into the earth to help ground and stabilize you. Use different colors, sizes, and textures to play with what feels right in any situation.

- Use a mantra or affirmation. Find a word, phrase, or prayer to center your mind and stay on track. A term such as *powerful*, *open*, or *breathe* or a phrase like "I am safe and trusting," "good vibes," or "the world is full of love" can all be gentle reminders of what you want your focus to be. Use that as your intention and focal point and return to it repeatedly, especially during periods of stress or chaos. This practice gives your brain something positive to think about and focus on. The brain can't stop thinking about something; it must start thinking about something else. Give it something positive to focus on.

- Dig in the dirt and walk barefoot on the ground.
- There is power in touch. It will help you ground and regulate energy. Carry a stone, coin, or marble in your pocket to give yourself a tactile grounding method and feel the energy of it. Hold something in your hand, rub it, and roll it around to channel the energy. Touch your wrists or thighs with a firm grip to feel different body parts, send energy through them, and get you back into your skin. Wring your hands, pinch your fingertips, and rub your hands down your arms and legs to move energy and be on touch with your body.
- Get outside and put your bare feet in the grass.

Visualization

The pictures in your head shape your reality, impacting how you feel and what you believe. Your brain cannot determine what's real and what isn't. It will believe whatever you tell it, look for evidence that it is true, and become well-rehearsed in what you focus on. I call this a "mental story." We mentally write them all the time, often with great detail without checking the facts or the health of them. The more emotion that surrounds your mental story, the more real and intense the story will be.

Just like children get pinched off from their intuition as they grow, creativity and imagination also become compromised. The tool of visualization allows you to play, dream, and explore with innovation and possibility.

Use visualization as often as you can. It's a fun, playful way to move energy, lighten emotion, and focus your attention. This is your path to creativity, clarity, and possibility. Create a picture or scene for your brain to home in on, then expand into it by adding specific details, emotions, and positive words to enhance your experience. Like you might begin with a blank print you start to add color to or a doodle that you find yourself adding dimension and detail to, so too can you explore within your imagination. The clearer your picture and the greater the emotion, the better. Allow yourself to play with images and scenarios to decide what feels best and aligns most with what you want to create.

Be as deliberate and intentional with the pictures, words, and phrases you use as you are with the dollars you spend or the food and drink you consume. Let go of labels, judgments, can'ts, shoulds, agendas, time frames, and doubts. If you're polluting your mind with such contaminated thoughts and ill-trained beliefs, then you must assess and consciously replace them as quickly and effectively as possible. Don't let negative thoughts linger too long; they gain momentum in a very short period of time. Never underestimate the power of the thoughts you entertain. The sky's the limit. Have fun, be childlike and curious as you experiment with your imagery.

Visualization will help you increase or move emotion and energy. It will allow you to ground and shift out of anything you don't want to experience or at least lighten the load of it. Use an array of pictures and techniques to modify the energy you experience to ignite the imagination and the power of the brain.

- Envision water, with its wavelike fluidity softening and flowing throughout your body to keep the energy in motion and release negativity or any sense that you're feeling "stuck."

- Imagine deep roots coming out of the bottom of your feet into the layers of the earth. You can send energy down and out where it can be reused and recycled for good. You can also use the depth of the roots to help you stay firmly grounded. These roots can be any color or texture you choose.

- Create a Vision Board and display it where you can see it consistently. Use it as a grounding reference point for what you want most in life. Be mindful and discriminating of any word or image you choose for your board.

- Visualize yourself surrounded with a layer of golden light. This helps protect what comes in and what goes out. You can retract or expand the thickness and texture of this based on how you feel and the situation you're in. Imagine that encompassing bright light as you go about your day to remind yourself of the protection you have and to manage what's yours and let go of what isn't.

- Surround others with a layer of golden light to allow them to manage what's theirs and to protect you from their energy. Visualize a large mirror that reflects any of their projections directly back to them.

- Imagine wrapping your loved ones in a blanket of light, love, or healing like you might swaddle an infant. Release them into the arms of their Divine Guidance so you can go about your business and know they are well cared for without your involvement.

- To help yourself detach from a situation or person, imagine sending their energy back to them. You can practice hitting the delete button, the send button, or stamping them with *Return to Sender* so they are left to deal with themselves, and you aren't so troubled by them or their circumstances.

- Separate your energy from others. As you leave an interaction or transition from one thing to the next, detach yourself and gather your energy back into yourself. Imagine "collecting your things" as you separate your energy from theirs.

- Visualize sweeping yourself off after an interaction or sweeping up the space around you to clear others' energy from the area.

- Picture a positive outcome and allow yourself to imagine how that success is going to feel.

- Imagine putting people or situations in a box both mentally and energetically to help you separate yourself. At any point, you can decide to get the box out, open it up, and manage whatever you need to manage inside of it. When you've spent all the time and energy you want to, lovingly put the top back on and put it away. If anything seeps out of it, remind yourself that it is safely tucked away in its proper place for now. This can be referred to as a God Box, Prayer Place, or Surrender Box.

Breath Work

This may seem like a silly reminder, but your first step in any of these practices is to breathe. Breath is life. It is the primary tool for moving you from fight or flight into a place of calm and reason. Use your breath to send energy in and out of your body and to manage tension and emotion. During times of turmoil, breathing may be very shallow as you tighten up and hold your breath. Use intentional breath to gain focus and clarity and to find your footing through deep belly breaths and cathartic exhales. Do this repeatedly until you feel a shift.

You can deliberately use your breath to calm or stimulate you. Slow, deep breaths will slow your heart rate and also gives you a soothing focal point to concentrate on. Rapid, heavy breathing will invigorate your system and ignite the fire within and stimulate energy.

- Use a Noticing Breath, one that allows you to observe yourself and your surroundings without judgment or expectation. Notice what's happening in and around you, without judgment or assessment, as you note any sensations or stories you're creating. You don't need to do anything; you're simply tuning in and paying attention to what *is* and how it impacts your body.
- Sigh deeply and heavily. Breathe in through your nose and let it out through your mouth in a long, vocal sigh. This is a great way to move energy out of your body. Exhale strongly, letting any heart or throat energy expel completely.
- Add a color to your breath and imagine it moving all through your body like a liquid dye. Lavender is calm and soothing versus fiery red to move frustration or anger.
- Send breath to others if you're feeling their energy. Steadily send energy back to them, visualizing the air gently returning to them as a means of detaching yourself.
- Make noise as you exhale, providing a further release. Hum, buzz, or yawn.
- Breathe in a positive word and feel its energy move through you.
- Picture breathing in love or peace and exhaling fear or fury.

- Visualize the toxicity moving out of your body as you expel breath. Imagine fire, dirt, bats, the color black—whatever helps you picture the toxicity leaving you. Move it out through your feet, your chest, or the top of your head.
- Regulate breath with inhaling to the count of four, holding for six, and exhaling for eight. You can change the numbers how you see fit; just exhale longer than you inhale.

Meditation

Remember, you don't have to look like an expert here, and there is no right way or wrong way to meditate. Any attempt at stillness and tuning in is beneficial.

- Quiet all sensory stimulation to create a soothing environment wherever possible. Recognize the impact of lights, noise, clutter, conversation, technology, etc., and do what you can to limit or alter these.
- Create a meditation spot of comfort, ease, and quiet. A closet, a corner, or an entire room can serve as a getaway that reinforces your permission to be still. Having an established area offers further permission and prompting to be still. It can also serve as a visual reminder for loved ones to leave you be while you're in there.
- Be present in your body and your experience in this moment. Take the time to feel into your current experience. Be where you are. Whatever you're doing, do only that. Focus and embrace your current circumstances (showering, eating, sitting still, brushing your teeth) to be more present in your life.
- Give your attention to just one thing. Home in on it, and when

you get distracted, refocus on that one thing. The supposed benefits of multitasking are a myth that adds unnecessary stress and divides your attention and presence.

- Make a list of priorities or to-dos to focus your attention and efforts. Use it as a focal point or anchor to keep yourself centered on what you are doing and what needs your attention. During times of stress or chaos, refer to your list and focus on the next right step.

- Set a timer for stillness and quiet. Two minutes or twenty, your mind, body, and spirit will benefit from consistent periods of rest and reset. Inspiration can easily be missed if you're flooded with busyness, noise, and distraction. Life will often prompt you quietly and gently. If your schedule, mind, and environment are jam-packed, consider emptying some physical, emotional, and energetic space to create room for deeper guidance. Pay attention to what comes up and what you're feeling when you get still and quiet. Stillness is a gift that may take some to get used to. Practice it.

- Follow along to a guided meditation. YouTube has a plethora that will open an entire world of different techniques, methods, and practices. Find one you like and look for similar styles to support your practice.

Movement

Physical movement changes your physical, emotional, and energetic state. The body endures, carries, and stores so much, and movement is a profound way to regulate and release. If you allow movement in any way or direction, the body will clearly show you the energy it's holding. That's why some people nervously tap, rock back and forth, or wring their hands. It's the body's way of trying to expel energy. A movement practice is a phenomenal way to not only shift energy, but to care for your body and have fun while you're doing it. The more you move, the more different you'll feel.

Suspend judgment, embarrassment, and fear as you tune in to your body and trust it to instinctively move the way it needs. Any type of movement to shift or shake your energy will be helpful. No one's watching, so move.

- Stretch, run, practice yoga, throw or kick a ball, walk, jump up and down, run up and down the stairs, dance, do some Qigong—just move!
- With her catchy tune, "Shake It Off," Taylor Swift was onto something. If you're feeling particularly funky, practice shaking it off. Have some fun, dance around, and move, move, move. Use your visualization tool to picture the release and disposal as you're literally shaking it off.
- Fiercely rub your hands together, feeling the energy and heat you're creating. Rub your palms over your face, through your hair, and around your skull.
- Roll your neck and shoulders or move them up and down rapidly.
- Attempt the Ecstatic Dance (which for some of us will be more like the Erratic Dance). Either way, play some music and allow yourself to move freely with the music.

Creativity and Expression

For this final tool, you may pick your potion: singing, dance, color, music, pottery, painting. Allow creativity to do the work for you without worrying about what it looks like. The goal is simply to create however the imagination wants. Stay away from judgment and simply allow energy to move through you in expressive ways. Allow childlike permission and freedom to have fun without attempts at perfection or pleasing others. Let go of outcomes and expectations and let curiosity and intuition do the work.

Some other creative ways to express yourself:

- Journaling—Your writing can be crafty and artistic or simply serve as a dumping ground for you to deposit negative energy. Putting pen to paper will allow you to get in touch with your inner thoughts. There's no need to focus on sentence structure, grammar, or punctuation; just get it out. Writing is a powerful activator to your subconscious and will shift your awareness to a different perspective and deeper level. Don't just think about it; write it out—and put pen to paper, not fingers to phone!
- Doodle—Get some markers or crayons and let loose. See what direction your intuition sends you when you allow your imagination to do the work.
- Do what fills your cup—nature, art, golf, travel, music, working out, painting, rest, gardening, kickboxing, comedy, etc. Do these as often as you can. Functioning from a full cup allows you to be aware, regulated, and relational.
- As we've seen, movement can be a highly expressive way to practice Embodiment and expression. Use your body to do the creative work through Embodiment practices, choosing any method you prefer.

THE UNIQUE PROCESS OF BUILDING INTUITION

Jan shared the importance of her spirituality, meditation, and reflection. I was curious and asked her about her practices and what she does to develop her relationship with who she referred to as God. She proceeded with a laundry list of items she used to receive messages and insight. She listed a prayer shawl she needed to wear along with her beads, crystals, and oils. She shared about her special candles that need to be lit in a certain order, and her specific prayer book she reads from. She may have recognized the dazed look in my eyes as she questioned, "What is it?"

Rituals and routines may help you develop a worship or stillness practice. You may feel spiritually connected with these instruments and feel good about implementing them into your routines. It's also important to recognize these are simply tools. You carry your intuition with you everywhere you go, and you're able to tap into it at any moment.

Like a muscle that can be strengthened and trained, your intuition benefits from consistent use and practice. Though your process for building your intuition will be as unique to you as Jan's was to her, the following practices can help build and intensify your instincts:

- **Listen to your body**—The body knows what's right for you and what isn't. It will intuitively determine something that's healthy versus that which isn't. If you investigate and inquire, it will properly and dependably inform you about what it needs.
- **GPS (Gut, Perception, and Senses)**—When you learn to inquire within, the body always knows what's in your best interest. Trust those intuitive nudges as they're offered. Tune in to, recognize, and honor what they're communicating. Commit

to following their direction, even when it doesn't immediately make sense.

- **Write**—Use pen and paper to explore your inner thoughts and feeling as often as you can. Every morning, write a few pages nonstop to see what needs to be purged and offered. You can purge the mental garbage that distracts you.
- **Meditate**—Little explanation is needed here. You know the importance of this tool. Still yourself long enough to pause and inquire within. Recognize any word or theme that surfaces. Have a journal handy to write down what's divulged.
- **Ask**—Feel free to ask any question you want to God, your spirit guides, ancestors, or angels. When things feel stressful or confusing, seek guidance and clarity by asking. Formulate questions in your writing and meditation and see what's revealed.

> *What am I supposed to be learning?*
> *What's the best option for me?*
> *Where should I go?*
> *What should I do?*
> *How can I serve?*
> *What's my highest and best?*

Write down the answers that arise, even if they don't make sense or you don't like what you're writing. A great time to do this is right after you awaken or right before bed.

Use the cluster technique that allows you to put a word in the middle of the page, and you simply write down whatever comes to mind—a story, memory, another word, or association. Allow the pen to be free flowing without judgment, assessment, or questioning. See what's revealed and allow the spirit to direct what you write.

- Put your hand over your Emotional Center and breathe into it, especially during stressful situations or when you're with intense, highly energetic people. Feel the beat of your heart and offer a calming word or phrase to ground and center yourself before you proceed. Tune in for intuitive nudges or gestures of how to cope and manage.

- **Slow down.** Take your time to assess situations, requests, or any type of decision. Just because someone has an immediate need does not mean you need to offer an immediate answer. Check in with yourself to see how you feel about something or someone before responding. Urgency and rushing imply fear or impulsivity, and a simple pause can offer much-needed time to gain perspective and assess intuitive responses. The intuition often waits for fear and frenzy to subside before "speaking."

- **Perform a consistent check-in during your day.** Pay attention to what you're thinking about to ensure you're powerfully aligned with something healthy and positive. Be conscious of worry, rumination, judgment, or lack. These will influence you more heavily than you realize. Thoughts matter greatly, as they shape your feelings and perspective. Clean up your energy and shift your focus as soon as you can so stress and negativity don't gain momentum.

- **Stillness, quiet, and solitude**—Allow room for your intuition to speak to you. Quiet the noise and develop a listening practice. Drive home in silence; sit still for a moment; do one thing at a time; get in the bathtub. These are all great examples of how to make room for insight.

- **Healthy sleep routine**—Always sleep in a dark, quiet, cool, tech-free zone. Incorporate white noise if needed. So much comes alive when your conscious mind is at rest. Sleep hygiene is as important as physical and emotional hygiene.

- **Keep a dream journal**—Dreams are your subconscious ways of speaking to you. Though they may be confusing, familiarizing yourself with themes, patterns, or feelings that surface from the dreams is an important practice. Invest in a quality dream dictionary and allow your intuition to clarify what is being communicated to you through your dreams. Note any patterns or themes that are consistent. Before drifting off to sleep, ask specific questions or present a situation in your journal. Write down anything your dreams offer when you wake up. Be careful not to grab for your phone or jump immediately out of bed. This will distract you from the restful state and jolt you into the hustle.

- **Rituals and routines**—Your morning and evening routines can be magical opportunities to summon spirit, focus and reflect on your day, and launch you into the next level. Pay close attention to how well those routines are serving you and aligning you with where you want to be emotionally and energetically.

What are your practices? Are you lost in the numbness of autopilot or caught in the rigidity and formalities of your habits? Create new routines—ones that start and end your day with calm, grounded focus that propels you into new levels of functioning.

Don't let yourself off the hook on this one with excuses and bad habits. Get up ten minutes early, lie in bed for three minutes to decide your daily mantra and politely greet the day, wait an hour before checking social media or email, and be intentional about your shower and hygiene as a grounding practice. Stop scrolling at least an hour before bed. Do the painstakingly right thing by breaking your bedtime television routine to fall asleep. Head to bed thirty minutes earlier than usual, even if you don't feel sleepy. Plug your phone in across the room. Yes, I know these practices may stink, but the costs and consequences of not doing them stink even more.

Each of these practices will help you direct your thoughts, feelings, and experiences. They will allow you to detach from others and find your footing so you can stay present and balanced. These are techniques to help you strengthen and align with your intuition. Take your time to familiarize yourself with these practices and the tools in the Empath's Toolbox to decipher which practice or tool is right for the job. You'll like some more than others, and certain tools will be more effective at different times. These are your tools to do with what you see as best.

INTUITION ASSESSMENT

I trust my intuition:

☐ RARELY   ☐ SOMEWHAT   ☐ COMPLETELY

I recognize intuitive nudges in the following ways:

1.
2.
3.

A specific time I trusted my intuition:

I'm comfortable spending time alone:

☐ RARELY   ☐ SOMEWHAT   ☐ COMPLETELY

I can tune in to my own voice and needs:

☐ RARELY   ☐ SOMEWHAT   ☐ COMPLETELY

A personal mantra I will incorporate:

Tools and practices I will engage in:

1.
2.
3.

CHAPTER 7

The Empowered Empath

You are allowed to be both a masterpiece and a work in progress, simultaneously.

—SOPHIA BUSH

There is no "right time." There is just time and what you choose to do with it.

—UNKNOWN

EMPOWERED—*"having the knowledge, confidence, means, or ability to do things or make decisions for oneself"*

—MERRIAM WEBSTER

Your belief system is the foundation for how you relate and function in the world. It shapes your outlook, perspective, and Sense of Self. As an Empath, you likely feel different—as though something is wrong or off about you. You may struggle with basic life tasks, feeling inept, insecure, and doubting yourself. Perhaps you've spent a great deal of time and effort trying to fit in, being chameleon-like, shapeshifting to fit your environment or meet others' expectations. You may have sought external approval and acceptance for a long time, always looking for assurance in the world, hyper-focused on others, accepting roles and responsibilities that command too much from you. As a result, you may have become a stranger to yourself.

So, let's get familiar with *you*. Sounds funny, doesn't it? At whatever age you are, with this chapter, we're going to explore your Sense of Self with a clean lens, newfound curiosity, and a friendly welcome. You're going to be clearing the slate and letting go of limiting stories and fictitious beliefs as you step into an empowered stance of living. This process is incredibly important, as it will set the foundation for the rest of the work you do.

WHO DO YOU THINK YOU ARE?

These words make me quake a bit, but I will pose the question again: *Who do you think you are?* How you answer is nothing short of life-defining. Can you feel the energy of that question in your body? Can you answer this with confidence, clarity, and assurance, knowing full well who you are and the gifts you carry in this world? Or are you someone who has learned to play small, fly under the radar, and please and appease others?

Remember, where you look is where you go. Where you choose to focus your attention is what will grow and be magnified. If you're looking at flaws, you'll see them in everything you do. Maybe you're someone who can easily rattle off their shortcomings and past mistakes, someone with a well-rehearsed story about being "less than."

Well, if this is you, then the story of unworthiness, dysfunction, and playing small ends here. Today, you claim your seat at the table of worthiness. If that makes you anxious, please remember that claiming your seat does not take space from someone else! It simply allows you to step into the place you belong, becoming who and what you were created to be.

If I asked you to make a list of your strengths and capabilities, would you be able to? Are you aware of your good parts as well as the not-so-good? What would it be like for you to lead with your strengths and claim your personal power? Are you willing to surrender the "less-than" story and begin a new script? This is your opportunity to move out from underneath the cloak of unworthiness and step into an empowered state.

"Know thyself" is some of Socrates's greatest wisdom. In this context, you're going to learn to value yourself, trust your body, know your truth, and value your instinct. All of this will deepen and strengthen your Sense of Self (SOS). You will use your gifts, wisdom, and personal truth to function from a place of strength and solidarity rather than subjecting yourself to the world at large and opinions of others. You will embrace the reality of who you are and prioritize yourself so you can be of greater service to yourself and others. It all begins with knowing who you are, what makes you tick, and what matters most to you.

This section affords you the space and permission to explore on a deeper level. The following exercises are intended for honesty and examination as you gain an empowered sense of who you are, what you're capable of, and what you believe in.

NAVIGATIONAL BEAMS

Your core values define what's important, worthy, and useful to you. They set the standard and direction for the decisions, relationships, and behaviors you adhere to in your daily life. In this way, they are like internal navigational beams that direct your course and determine what you say yes or no to. So, if you can develop a crystal clear focus on your core values, it will empower you by creating alignment in your thoughts, words, and deeds.

What do you value the most? It's an important question that few ever take the time to answer or truthfully determine. Most people are unaware, too busy, or assume they know what their values are. Have you settled into what you were taught or role modeled without questioning what's true for you? Maybe you've allowed your core values to be dictated to you, rather than taking the time to explore and define them for yourself. Have you dug deep enough to reckon with anything more than generalized values of family, world peace, or God? Have you let yourself off easy by going with superficial or standard priorities of what you think you *should* value?

So, I'll ask you again, *What do you value the most?* What kind of person are you, and what are your priorities? Asking these questions opens the opportunity to identify and define your core values. Be honest and allow yourself to investigate your driving forces. There are no right or wrong. These are yours to define and claim.

THE CORE VALUES EXERCISE

Years ago, when I was creating this exercise, a disturbing truth surfaced. For most of my life, I declared *kindness* as one of my core values. I'm an Empath and a social worker, for goodness' sake! I care deeply about people. Yet, my thoughts and feelings were often riddled with judgment, impatience, fury, and intolerance, and I often felt very unkind. If I really valued kindness, why was I feeling so ruthless?

As I sat with this exercise I was creating for clients, I challenged myself to clear my own lens, reset my thinking, and get honest about what I *actually* value. What came forth was astounding to me. The good news is, I really do value kindness, but the reality is, it didn't even make my top ten. Quite a humbling experience.

For the first time ever, I learned that what I really value is *fairness*. I was kind when people were kind and situations were pleasant. When I found people to be rude, difficult, or hurtful, kindness seemed to slip out the back. It's not a core value if you only feel it in certain situations. For me this was a *redefining* experience, but I had to be honest and dig deep beyond what I had allowed myself to believe for many years.

The most powerful starting point for determining your core values is to ask yourself who you want to be in the world. What contribution do you want to make? Next, ask what types of relationships you want to have. There are no right or wrong answers; your core values are as unique and personal as your fingerprints. Self-honesty, self-defining, and self-referencing are essential tools in this process.

Further, it's important to assess your behavior and attitude. These are also reflective of your values. Because of the roles I played and who I *wanted* to be, I believed kindness was core. However, a humbling self-assessment such as this one allowed me to address my actions and approach, revealing a deeper truth about myself.

Let's begin your core values exercise. First, go through the following list and mark each value that resonates with you. Highlight anything that feels important. Please don't mark these off based on what you think you *should* value, old thoughts about what you value, or anything related to what other people might think of you. Focus on what *feels* right without overthinking. Trust the way the words feel when you read them. There is no limit to the number of words you can identify. You might mark one or two, and you might mark fifty.

Abundance	Contribution	Harmony
Acceptance	Contentment	Health
Accountability	Courage	Helping
Achievement	Creativity	Home
Adventure	Curiosity	Honesty
Advocacy	Decisiveness	Hope
Appreciation	Dependability	Humility
Authenticity	Dignity	Humor
Autonomy	Diversity	Inclusion
Balance	Efficiency	Independence
Beauty	Empathy	Influence
Being the best	Environment	Innovation
Belonging	Ethics	Intelligence
Bravery	Excellence	Integrity
Calm	Excitement	Intuition
Career	Expressiveness	Joy
Caring	Fairness	Justice
Challenge	Faith	Kindness
Community	Family	Knowledge
Commitment	Finances	Leadership
Compassion	Freedom	Learning
Competence	Friendship	Legacy
Competition	Fun	Leisure
Confidence	Future Generations	Love
Connection	Generosity	Making a difference
Cooperation	Grace	Mindfulness
Collaboration	Growth	Nature
Consistency	Happiness	Openness

Optimism	Risk-taking	Thoughtfulness
Order	Safety	Thrift
Parenting	Security	Time
Patriotism	Serenity	Tradition
Peace	Self-Discipline	Travel
Perseverance	Self-Expression	Trust
Personal	Self-Respect	Truth
Development	Simplicity	Understanding
Power	Spirituality	Uniqueness
Pride	Sportsmanship	Usefulness
Recognition	Stability	Vision
Relationships	Stewardship	Wealth
Reliability	Status	Well-being
Respect	Success	Whole-Hearted
Resourcefulness	Teamwork	Wisdom
Responsibility	Thankfulness	Work

After you have finished checking your words, go through the list again. This time, limit your focus to *three* words that you value most. These will be your core values.

Now, if narrowing it down to three is too big of a leap on this round, then narrow it down to ten, then move to five, and then choose three. If you're having trouble arriving at that final number, just imagine a strong wind comes along, and you can grab hold of just three. Prioritizing these three values doesn't eliminate the others. You can keep as many *general* values as you prefer, but for the sake of determining *core* values, let's concentrate on these three to gain clarity and focus.

These core values serve as an anchor. They will always be your home base. When things get difficult, you doubt yourself, or tension mounts and conflict arises, your core values will be your grounding and reference points, your true north. They will enable you to stay the course and remember what's important to you as you move deeper into this work.

NOTES:

My three core values are:

1.

2.

3.

Other people's opinions weighed heavily in my assessment.

☐ NOT AT ALL   ☐ SOMEWHAT   ☐ VERY MUCH

I noticed *should* thinking when trying to decide. I felt concerned about what was "right" rather than what was important to me.

☐ NOT AT ALL   ☐ SOMEWHAT   ☐ VERY MUCH

My core values are evident in the way I conduct myself.

☐ NOT AT ALL   ☐ SOMEWHAT   ☐ VERY MUCH

My thoughts and words are aligned with my top values.

☐ NOT AT ALL   ☐ SOMEWHAT   ☐ VERY MUCH

I use my core values in decision-making and determining my course of action.

☐ NOT AT ALL   ☐ SOMEWHAT   ☐ VERY MUCH

IT'S A CLUSTER!

Imagine going through life believing that 1 + 1 = 3. You can see the mistakes you would make in everyday life having drawn such a faulty conclusion. Have you ever stopped to consider other conclusions you've drawn? Do you take the time to assess the accuracy and quality of your thoughts and beliefs? Have you ever considered thinking about what you're thinking about? This is your opportunity to ponder your assumptions about yourself, other people, success, love, happiness, the rest of the world, your worthiness, and so on.

Until this day, your subconscious belief system has set the tone for how you have shown up in the world and the expectations you have held for yourself and others. The subtle conclusions you've unknowingly made have established a foundation for your beliefs, emotions, and behaviors. They have influenced the way you see yourself and the rest of the world. This is part of why the core values exercise can be so surprising. Perhaps you've built your foundation on faulty suppositions without even being aware.

There are tools and resources for exploring your inner beliefs to see how well they're serving you. One way to tap into the subconscious quickly and easily is to use a tool I refer to as *cluster work*. A cluster is a writing brainstorm that allows freedom and permission to explore your beliefs and associations with everyday concepts such as love, success, happiness, family, etc. You can gain a lot of clarity using this technique.

Cluster work is a creative way to become aware of your subconscious beliefs, assess those beliefs, and then clarify your opinions and viewpoints from a free-flowing train of thought. It's an opportunity to explore and express yourself without filters or judgment, a powerful tool that reveals layers of subconscious information that are worth conscious attention.

Clustering is simple. You write a word at the top or in the middle of a page and then let your intuition and pen do the rest. For example, write the word *love* in the middle of a blank page and see what's revealed as you release the thoughts, feelings, and memories you associate with the word.

It's incredibly important to allow your body and your heart to do this work. Don't get caught up in your head, worrying about what you should or shouldn't write. Clustering is free flowing, so allow yourself the freedom to explore and investigate your inner world without judgment or expectation.

If you want to probe even deeper, use crayons, markers, paints, and colored pencils to activate profound creativity and insight. Allow your instinct and intuition to guide you to specific colors or textures that will emphasize what's surfacing. If you need to, invest in an extra-large artist's notebook for room to expand and explore further.

This technique allows you to dig deep into your subconscious and clear out old beliefs, unsupportive opinions, and faulty ideas. Many of these patterns are hidden, yet they serve as an undercurrent for your present living. Clustering allows you to see these patterns in plain sight so that you can revamp and reset them with intention and improvement.

Let's get to the basics. The words "I am" are two of the most important words you can utter. What you believe to be true about yourself will shape what you think, how you act, the people you associate with, and what you tolerate. Your "I am" statements reveal your beliefs and create the foundation for everything you say, do, and allow.

As you move further into the work of an Empowered Empath, it's essential to formulate healthy, productive "I am" statements. But first, let's explore what's inside you today, at the start of your journey, so you can address what needs to be cleaned up, healed, or let go of.

In the middle of the page, write the words *I am*. What immediately comes to mind? What thoughts, words, or memories surface? Allow all of those words to fall onto the paper. Remember, no judgment or criticism. This is for assessment and awareness only.

I am

Know thyself.

—SOCRATES

This exercise revealed:

1.

2.

3.

The critical "I ams" I want to release are:

1.

2.

3.

The empowering "I ams" I want to practice and build upon are:

1.

2.

3.

Healthy, clear, strong "I ams" lay the foundation for the enlightened work you're called to do. Just as you've practiced those gentle emotional shifts we addressed in chapter two, so too can you practice shifting and improving your belief systems.

If you're dead broke, telling yourself, "I am a millionaire" will register as BS to every system in your body. A gentle shift such as, "I am making better choices every day" will be more digestible and believable. If you've had one poor relationship after another, saying, "I am happily committed to my forever partner" will be hard to swallow. More accurate, digestible statements would be, "I am worth knowing," or, "I have friends and family who love me dearly," or "I am loveable."

Commit to these gentle shifts and more accurate, digestible statements, and they will serve as a launching pad for even stronger "I ams." Put another way, don't try to feed yourself something that's not believable yet. You have to work your way up, gently, and consistently improving and escalating what you're allowing yourself to believe.

It's important to meet yourself on the positive side of where you are rather than at some lofty, fabricated affirmation that doesn't suit you. Meanwhile, never entertain a negative "I am." Uttering words of shame, judgment, and ridicule are self-betraying and do nothing to serve you. Make your "I ams" positive, affirming, believable, and kind.

"I am" phrases that are manageable and feel good:

1.

2.

3.

Things I appreciate about me:

1.

2.

3.

4.

5.

6.

7.

8.

9.

10.

STEPS FOR EMPOWERED LIVING

1. **Practice**—Choose an empowered "I am" and practice it for a period of time. See what happens. Are you able to incorporate the belief and buy into it fairly easily? Is it starting to feel more real and comfortable?

    Create a new "I am" every day as your mantra and grounding force and try it on for size. Make sure it's an uplifting, positive one. Have fun with this. Use it as your daily affirmation to create a continual positive loop in your mind and self-talk. Then, tomorrow, try a new one on for size. Today can be "I am playful." Tomorrow can be "I am filled with positive energy." Try them all on for size. Some will fit comfortably, some you may have to stretch into, and others won't fit at all. You get to decide.

    Develop a routine of repeating and rehearsing your "I am" mantra when you're in the shower, drinking your coffee, or doing a movement practice. This will solidify it into a normalized way you see and refer to yourself.

    What stories, resistance, or fears surface when you think about your "I am" mantra? Can you notice those thoughts without caving into the pressure of them? Does your inner critic rear its ugly head?

    Make a list of other beliefs or affirmations you want to adopt, and practice each of them consistently. Just like a muscle, you'll adapt and strengthen in specific areas that are right for you.

2. **Posture and Eye Contact**—You can tell a lot about someone by the way they carry and conduct themselves. Be mindful

of your posture, stance, eye contact, and the firmness of your handshake. These matter and convey energy.

Hunched shoulders, scattered or evasive eye contact, looking down, and whispering tones don't serve you or align with empowerment. You don't need to be extreme, wave a banner, stand on a soapbox, or hold a megaphone, but be mindful of how you enter a room and the way your nonverbal behaviors speak for you.

3. **Act As If**—This is an incredibly effective tool, not only in changing your mindset but in aligning your behavior with who you want to be and what you want to accomplish. This practice integrates small steps supporting where you want to go, like mile-markers along the way ensuring you're heading in the right direction.

This tool has allowed me and many of my clients to dig through situations we couldn't muster all at one time and never thought possible to accomplish. One step at a time, you take action toward something you want to achieve. Maybe you don't do anything else for months, but there is a willingness and steadfastness to move forward as you're ready, in the direction you want to go. With the gifts of intuition and all of the empowering tools you're learning, you continue along your designated path.

Let's say you want to go back to school but can't imagine how to do so. Your mind focuses on dozens of reasons you could never do it. But as you practice the Acting As If steps, you become curious about the possibility and open yourself up to the idea.

You get online and search graduate programs (Acting As If step #1). You email a few schools for information about a specific program that interests you (Acting As If step #2). You schedule a call with the head of the program to ask questions about returning students (Acting As If step #3). You plan a visit to the campus (Acting As If step #4).

Little steps all along the way make the process more manageable. The best news: there's no harm or risk in any of these steps. You're simply opening to possibilities. If you change your mind, become uninterested, or decide the time isn't right, there's no problem. All you're doing is seeking information, asking questions, and having conversations. No harm, no foul. You don't have to commit to anything, sign any papers, or put down any money. You're taking this one step at a time to see what's possible.

As you move forward, the Acting As If stages will require more commitment or action from you, but you can handle those as you go along. Equally, you can always change your mind or slow the process. This is all up to you.

4. **Make Your Values Visual**—Now that you have identified and accepted your three core values, visually incorporate them into your daily life. Put them on sticky notes, make them screen savers, write them in your journal or planner, draw them on the bathroom mirror in dry erase, print them off and use them on your Vision Board.

Train your brain to be deeply rooted in what's important to you. If you have conflict with someone or are trying to make a decision about something, use your core values as the filters through which you decide.

❧ EMPOWERED LIVING

To me, living an empowered life means:

1.

2.

3.

Obstacles or struggles I've had with living an empowered life include:

1.

2.

3.

Because I am living an empowered life, I will:

1.

2.

3.

Action steps I'm ready to take to life an empowered life include:

1.

2.

3.

PERSONAL LEARNING:

CHAPTER 8

Expression

And the day came when the risk to remain tight in a bud
was more painful than the risk it took to blossom.

—ANAÏS NIN

EXPRESSION—*"the process of making known one's thoughts or feelings"*

—OXFORD LANGUAGES

O livia knew she was an Empath before she entered my office. She had spent years doing self-help work, exploring the many layers of the therapeutic onion, and yet was paralyzed by conflict. She suffered from horrible mood swings, somatic symptoms, and a passive approach to relationships. Having the information and knowledge wasn't leading to a better life or symptom relief in the way she expected.

She shared in detail the classic deer-in-the-headlight response she experienced when someone was upset, even if that person wasn't upset with her. Whenever this happened, Olivia found that she couldn't formulate words, take action, assert, honor, or protect herself. She felt frozen when someone was heated, loud, angry, or animated in any way. It was as if years of stifled emotion were trapped in her body, resulting in chronic aches and pains, throat issues, and a neck and shoulders so tense that she visited her chiropractor more often than she saw her closest friends. The anxiety and physical pain of not addressing these issues was evident, but she had no idea what to do or where to start.

Like a physical trainer would start you with a modest regimen of two- or five-pound weights as you began your fitness journey, so too did I start Olivia with small, manageable strategies for her to address her feelings and find her voice. There was a serious disconnect between her head, heart, and voice, so tuning her into emotions and physical cues was the first step as she learned to recognize and honor specific reactions, using them as indicators and cues that needed some attention.

She started so small, she could hardly notice a difference: asking a stranger to pass the salt when she previously would not have "bothered" them, telling a telemarketer she wasn't interested rather than listening to the entire pitch and feeling obligated to invest, and taking a walk down the street to introduce herself to a neighbor who recently moved in. She practiced in ways that felt manageable and positive and helped her build awareness, confidence, and assurance. Any time she felt the slightest nudge, she took some small action.

Slowly but surely, pieces of Olivia's rigid, fearful self began to relax and loosen as she became more comfortable with the smaller steps. She began to increase her personal growth and try different challenges that intimidated and scared her a little. She quickly learned where energy collected within her body and sought various movement and breath techniques when emotion felt bigger than she was used to handling. Step by step, she walked through the discomfort and uncertainty of harder, scarier opportunities to assert herself and communicate her feelings, needs, and preferences.

Olivia familiarized herself with her personal cues and indicators that emotion and energy were clogging up, or a decision was brewing, or conversation needed to be had. Over time, she learned to be direct, expressive, and clear with the others. She became more confident, assured, and though conflict was never her favorite, she felt capable of navigating those waters with people for the first time in her life.

Uncomfortable with the changes Olivia was making, some friends faded away—but only the ones who previously benefited from her passivity and over-functioning, the folks who couldn't or wouldn't hear or share with her. These changes were necessary, but they came with a sense of loss and disappointment, so it took some time for Olivia to process and grieve. Moving forward, she was very intentional with whom and how she engaged, and soon enough, she found herself being a welcomed part of a healthier, happier community of safe, quality people.

WHAT IS *EXPRESSION*?

Silenced, shut down, ridiculed, made fun of, confused, constrained, misunderstood . . . None of these are foreign to an empathic spirit. The world is intense—so intense that it can be hard for Empaths to be in it, much less navigate it effectively. Interacting, relating, and connecting to others can be challenging, while energetic overload can leave you exhausted and depleted. Meanwhile, being tender-hearted may leave you susceptible to absorbing emotion and energy while gathering in your mind, body, and spirit.

With all of this in mind, the term *expression* in this context refers to the ability to find your voice and move energy out and through your body.

In this chapter, you'll learn techniques and practices that allow you to be present in any experience with the ability to process what's happening and decide how you want to deal with it most effectively. This can be an outward, verbal, or physical expression, such as a conversation, sigh, or an act of movement. Or it can be a mental or emotional shift that is a more intimate, internal process, such as an affirmation, setting an intention, or repeating a mantra.

We've shared that energy and emotion can clog, collect, and gather in ways that can wreak havoc. Expression includes the methods, tools, and practices to move energy and emotion, shifting and directing it in a fashion that stabilizes and empowers you. It's the skillful nature of acknowledging your experience: "I'm really overwhelmed"; clarifying your needs: "I need some rest and refocus"; and aligning with a healthy course of action: "I'm heading home early tonight to get a good dinner, take a walk, and get myself to bed by ten."

Expression can include voicing words you previously would've stifled and swallowed, or an embodied practice that enables you to move and release energy, such as breath work or journaling, or a specific act or gesture that allows you to be seen or heard, like calling a friend to vent and brainstorm, when you typically would've faded into the background. This process enables you to express emotions, needs, and energy directly and effectively rather than stifling, suppressing, clogging up, or exploding.

Expression is like recycling. Rather than allowing all that energy to pile up and cause a mess or go unused, these practices enable you to repurpose what you're experiencing for a greater good. Finding ways to release or redirect energy and emotion can be a beautiful way to nurture and honor your empathic wiring.

EXPRESS YOURSELF

What is your response to conflict, hurt feelings, confusion, or difficult conversations? What are your strategies for handling something or someone that needs to be addressed? When you have a reaction or big feelings about something that's happened, what are some of your coping mechanisms? Do you know how to express yourself effectively? Are you confident in the words you speak and the way you interact with others? When conflict or difficulties arise, can you clarify your needs and assert your voice? When you have a need, feel vulnerable, or have made a mistake, how do you manage the susceptibility of those experiences? Can you be authentic and true to yourself? When you start to notice emotional issues surfacing, do you know how to move energy through your body and manage them to avoid overwhelm, absorption, or depletion?

Learning to address conflict or difficult circumstances is essential for your well-being. You may have developed longstanding patterns of denial, avoidance, suppression, self-shaming, submission, and silence. You may react, explode, and be highly defensive. Perhaps you harbor deep resentments about things you don't know how to express. Patterns such as these will fester and serve as emotional cancers that impact you, others, the quality of relationships, your emotional state, and simply make hard situations much worse.

Expression is highly individualized. You will have your own methods, timing, and preferences for knowing how to say or release what you need to. This practice incorporates many different approaches, along with a keen awareness of how to act in your own best interest. You can become skilled and capable at navigating harder issues, difficult conversations, and deep emotions.

Expression is not a verbal attack, nor does it have to be an eloquent conversation. It's simply your ability to speak up when you need to or to move emotion and energy effectively through your body to prevent clogging and contamination. It can be a word like "ouch" or a phrase like "That's not okay with me" or "I see it differently." It can be a long letter you intend to send or a venting session written in your journal that's never intended for another soul. It can be a raging dance in the middle of your office behind closed doors or a gentle sway of movement when you're waiting impatiently. It can be a good hard cry in the shower or a shovel in the backyard you use to dig out your hurt and fury. Expression can look like anything you want it to, as long as you are shifting and moving energy in a productive way.

CORE HUMAN NEEDS

To be *seen* . . . This is perhaps one of the most terrifying human needs, and yet, we all experience it, the need to be seen. To be seen, to be heard, to be known, to matter. There is great power and vulnerability in each of these core needs. Connection, mattering, and belonging are fundamental to our well-being. Your core needs drive your behavior, moods, and responses. They also come out sideways if you don't understand what they are or how to recognize them.

As an Empath attuned to the feelings and needs of others, it may not have occurred to you to tune in and honor *your* needs first. Expression is a powerful starting point as you become conscious and aware of your body and offer self-permission to explore and make space for your feelings and needs. Further, it allows you to regulate and develop effective strategies for meeting your needs. You're able to speak up, make effective decisions, cry when you need to, and redecide when appropriate.

Expression is your ability to act in your best interest with a consistent practice of showing up for yourself in an empowered way as you move and release energy and emotion. It helps you remain steadfast, grounded, and fully embodied as you open yourself to people, situations, and practices that meet your need to be seen, heard, known, and to matter. It's a level of confidence and assurance that you can take care of what needs to be taken care of in ways that are self-honoring and self-respectful.

You are unique, and your gifts, when used properly, will strengthen you and influence others in profound ways. You are much needed on this earth, yet you can only serve when you're at your strongest and healthiest. Otherwise, you're not helping in healthy ways. Expression is a vital process that will keep you healthy, happy, and strong.

Corinna was a business coach who came to me for coaching. Networking was a necessary part of building her business, getting referrals, and sharing her passion. One problem: she hated it. She would often sign up for events but couldn't bring herself to go. Or worse, she would plaster on that horribly fake smile, rigidly shake hands in the politest fashion she could muster, and rehearse her two-minute elevator pitch ad nauseam until she found the first opportunity to exit stage left. She would leave feeling exhausted, awkward, and defeated every time.

Because she didn't feel comfortable in her own skin at events that were critical for her business, Corrina believed herself destined to fail. She'd been holding on to subconscious fears and limiting beliefs—so much so that she thought the imposter syndrome was written solely about her. She just *knew* at any moment these professionals would call her out for being a fake and a phony. She worked in an industry that required her to be front and center on a regular basis, and yet she was terrified to be seen.

Paradoxically, she knew exactly what to tell her coaching clients to do, but when it came to her own fear and doubt, she felt almost paralyzed by the hypocritical nature of her practice. As an Empath, she was well versed at showing up the way she was expected to, but that presence was inauthentic and hurting the way she showed up professionally.

Our initial work centered around awareness and experimentation. Corrina was able to see clearly how much she was working to please and perform for others. Her instinct was to soak up the energy of the room and those around her and try to alter herself and her message to suit everyone else. She was trying to be liked and make an impression rather than being grounded, trusting the process, and enjoying herself.

Our next phase of work focused on education about her patterns, along with the tools and methods of expression. She was fascinated by the new lens of seeing herself and her experiences and quickly discovered several practices she enjoyed and found highly effective at moving and managing energy. Grounding, breath work, gentle movement, specific items she held in her hand, and visualization allowed her to be present at these events and speak from the inside out, sharing genuinely about the work she offered, and more importantly, who she was as a person.

Awareness, coupled with practices of expression, gave Corrina access to tools to manage her experiences differently. She was able to let go of those performance and pleasing modes and not be an emotional sponge, which in turn allowed her to show up authentically and enjoy getting to know others and share her passion for the work she does.

Years later, I attended a local networking event, and my conversations with Corrina pleasantly came to mind as I wondered how she was doing after all this time. Upon entering the building, I was snapped back into reality when I recognized my own need to breathe, center, and ground when I felt the surge of energy and commotion. The room was buzzing, the conversations were loud, and as I made my way through the crowd, an intriguing woman caught my focus. She was beaming with confidence and authenticity. It took me a moment, but quickly it clicked that the captivating woman was Corrina. Certainly, this was not the same woman who entered my office years ago, but a stronger, more confident version of her. I could sense and see how comfortable she was, having stepped into her own power.

It must've been an energetic thing, because her eyes drifted from her conversation and immediately met mine. As I clicked into focus for her, her face brightened, and she excused herself. We embraced quickly with kind regard, and she spilled forth with all her progress and success, though she needed no words to explain as the change was so evident.

That old playbook of pleasing and performing had been shredded as she shared about her new processes, rituals, and sense of empowerment. She was genuine and assured of her strengths and capabilities. She knew how to ground herself to detach and deflect energy. She was confident in who she was and what she had to offer the world. She was aligned with her core purpose and values and took nothing personally about where connections were or were not made. It seemed as if I was interacting with an entirely different person, and the change in her was strong and solid.

We got one final laugh as she excitedly said, "Oh, wait . . . you'll love this" and reached into her pocket and pulled out a shell she had chosen as one of her original grounding tools. I didn't say a word as I reached into my pocket and pulled out the rock I used for my own grounding work. The smiles we exchanged were ones of deep gratitude and admiration for the power of this work. I look forward to the possibility of seeing her again at future events.

EMBODIED EXPRESSION

Embodied expression is the free-flowing release of emotion and energy that allows you to reset and renew as needed. It's the ability to tune in and determine the right course of action. This tool grants you permission to play and explore with various methods and techniques to see what serves you best and is most effective.

Children are wonderful teachers of this process, and they're fun to learn from as you explore your practice of expression. Think about a child who flits about without a care of how they look or what people think of them. Kids go about their business with a spirit of innocence and ease. They cry when something hurts their feelings, then burst into spontaneous laughter when something tickles their funny bone. They give no regard to the latest fashion trends and know nothing of race, religion, politics, or gender. There are no rigid deadlines, pressures to be perfect, or rules about achievements and performance. Their play is not laced with hidden agendas, fierce competition, or deep-seated insecurities. They simply play for one purpose: pleasure.

Of course, as adults, we have obligations and responsibilities. Yes, you need to be mindful of your surroundings, and there are rules and social guidelines that allow for collective gathering, but Empaths often take these notions too far and become riddled with the pressures, demands, and expectations of the world, pinching themselves off from play, spontaneity, and fun. In recognizing this tendency, you can turn to expression as a tool that allows you to reintroduce play, creativity, and movement to release energy and realign you with your body.

Much like the play of an innocent child who is simply expressing and exploring, so too can you learn methods and strategies for experiencing life. Expression can take the form of a simple act of self-care, a conversation, or a public display or offering. The key is to find your voice, utilize your body, and engage in some of the practices in the next section to purposefully move energy through you to keep it fluid and flowing the way it's intended.

There's an authenticity to expression that allows the practices you choose to genuinely become your own. Establishing your preferred practices allows you to tap into freedom and ease, opening you up to effectively move energy and regulate your experiences. Yoga is a body, mind, and spirit example of expression for me. My mat becomes my playground for expression, utilizing movement, release, breath work, grounding, exploration, play, and personal challenge. What's a method you're willing to explore?

EXPRESSION PRACTICES

Embodied expression is not a performance or intended to serve anyone but you. You decide what feels right and what methods serve you best. There's no prize or reward waiting for you at the end of the day for the ways you've executed any type of expression. You can't do this wrong; it doesn't matter what others think. This is *your* practice of moving energy and managing your emotion to the best of your ability so that it doesn't clog or fester inside of you. Have fun, be playful, and honor that incredible voice you've been given.

Physical Movement:
There's a lot of power in moving the body in many capacities—fast, slow, frantic, fierce, methodical. Movement is a wonderful strategy for deliberate expression. It can be a consistent practice or random acts,

such as chopping vegetables, digging into the dirt to plant something, or spastic dance moves to help you shake it all off. These are intentional acts that help move and shift energy.

Dance	Stretch	Punch	Shake
Dig	Yoga	Qigong	Walk
Run	Chop	Shower	Climb stairs
Hug	Yard Work	Hike	Walk barefoot
Clean	Jump up & down		

Breath:

Belly Breathing is a technique that allows you to move breath deep into your belly to use your entire torso to experience the power of breath. It also allows you to draw breath up and in from the belly, depending on which direction you feel the most benefit.

Lion's Roar is an expressive, cathartic way of releasing air and moving energy like the roar of the fierce cat, while Alternate Breathing is closing off one nostril to take in air, closing off the opposite nostril to release it as a way of using both sides of the brain to reregulating yourself.

Sigh	Sing	Hum	Buzz	Belly Breathing
Lion's Roar		Alternate Nostril Breathing		

Stillness:

Prayer	Mindfulness	Repeat a Mantra
Rest	Meditation	Walking Meditation
Sitting	Kundalini Yoga	Visualization

Creativity:

Anything can be a canvas for you to explore your originality and vision. Use any of these methods to tap into your imagination, inspiration, and intuition. Free flow without overthinking, perfectionism, judgment, or criticism.

Draw	Paint	Color	Clay	Write	Sing
Dance	Doodle	Sketch	Poetry	Crochet	Cook
Pastels	Inks	Improv	Blog	Craft a story	

Experiment with makeup   Paint furniture   Bullet Journal

Move furniture around   Photography   Vision Boards

Repurpose household items   Scrapbooking   Style your hair

Words:

Words matter and they carry energy. There are the words you speak and words you think. There are well-practiced scripts that have likely become part of your consistent dialogue. Every word you utter and allow to enter your mind influences your mood, outlook, and perspective. Take time to think about what you're thinking about and make a commitment to choose your words and thoughts carefully.

Affirmations	Mantra	Prayer	Compliments
Journal	Cluster	Poetry	Song writing

Letter writing—*to send or to simply process your thoughts*

Words are a vital part of expression—whether it be the words you are speaking to yourself or to others, about yourself or about others, or regarding circumstances and situations. What you say and how you say it weighs heavily into the health and quality of your perspective, relationships, and experiences; however, you might not know what to say. Finding your voice in challenging situations may take some time and practice. Remember the "Acting As If" tool as you consider the examples below.

A simple, yet firm phrase allows you to acknowledge your experience without getting too far into the weeds or in over your head with something you don't feel ready for. These are the baby steps of expression.

"Ouch!"

"Wow!"

"I love spending time together like this."

"I need some time to process that."

"Sounds like you've got a lot of ideas."

"That's something I disagree with."

"I see things differently."

"I'll give that some thought."

Expression is vital, as well as personal and intimate. Your techniques will vary, as will your needs. Take your time. Practice different techniques. Be willing to take a risk and feel a bit uncomfortable. You're worth it!

EXPRESSING EMPATHY

PERSONAL LEARNING:

I'm able to express myself effectively.

☐ NOT AT ALL ☐ SOMEWHAT ☐ VERY MUCH

When it comes to conflict, I can handle myself well.

☐ NOT AT ALL ☐ SOMEWHAT ☐ VERY MUCH

Issues or people I have a hard time expressing myself with include:

1.
2.
3.

I am ready and willing to address the following issues:

1.
2.
3.

Methods of expression I'm willing to practice:

1.

2.

3.

I have a community of people who honor and respect me as I am.

☐ NOT AT ALL   ☐ SOMEWHAT   ☐ VERY MUCH

Some activities or adventures I feel curious about and am willing to try:

1.

2.

3.

Some things I'd like to learn more about:

1.

2.

3.

PERSONAL LEARNING:

CHAPTER 9

Endings

---

*There is no real ending. It's just the place where
you stop the story.*

—FRANK HERBERT

"How is it I've worked my entire life to get to this point, and now I'm more lost than I've ever been?" Shannon asked me shortly after her retirement.

Meanwhile, Joe spent weeks sorting through his reaction to a recent breakup. "I've wanted to break up with her for months. Why am I so devastated?"

"My kids are all happy, exactly where they want to be in life, and I could walk to their houses right down the road. Why does my heart hurt so much?" Even Linda's husband couldn't understand her reaction to the kids finally being out of the house.

Endings . . . they have a certain feel to them, don't they? They're sad but not always; sometimes they're confusing, relieving, and necessary. An ending is defined as a final part of something. Also, a termination of a state or situation. It's final, done, closed, over.

Whether we're talking about Empaths or otherwise, I don't think we as a culture give enough attention or permission for people to feel into their endings. Graduation days, retirement, marriages, births, empty nesting—these are typically well celebrated and acknowledged. Each is a new chapter, a defining point in someone's life story. Divorces and breakups are so commonplace that people rarely give the space needed to process, heal, and readjust from such huge transitions. Even if the separation is necessary or long overdue, it can be a death of sorts. There is energy and finality around endings that deserve your attention and recognition to process how you feel and give you room and permission to adapt and to define what this experience means to you.

Endings need a little breathing room to see where the pieces are going to land and how you want to move forward. Regardless of the specific details of the ending or change, there are lessons to be learned, feelings needing to be felt, and new meanings to be found. People tend to minimize, rush, numb, busy themselves, and distract through ending experiences. Loss has been normalized to the point of irrelevance. Enduring change or loss is different from embracing it. Trying to escape, excuse, rush through, or logically explain what you're going through will leave fragmented pieces that likely splinter in other areas of your life.

Proper endings create the necessary healing and space to launch powerful beginnings. Time spent in grief, reflection, or adjustment is never wasted time. Think of the magic that happens during the dead of winter. Spring could never happen without the metaphorical mortality of fall and the bitter coldness of winter. These seasons (whether in life or in the world around us) are necessary and valuable. They allow you to clean up and put things to rest appropriately so that you can move into the next season.

NECESSARY CHANGES / NECESSARY LOSSES

Nate worked with me off and on for years, often restarting his work after the holidays when there had been yet another family crisis. The holidays were approaching, and he knew he did not want to spend one more disastrous evening picking up the pieces of his destructive, chaotic relatives. It was time to do something different. Yet, he had no idea where to begin or how to deal with the repercussions of creating the changes he needed to make. This course of work was to be his deepest.

For weeks he came in questioning, "Am I really going to break up with my family?" "What kind of person leaves his parents alone during the holidays?" "What are people going to say about me?" The voices in his head were as daunting as the decisions he was contemplating. There were changes Nate needed to make, boundaries he had to set for his sanity and well-being, and behaviors he wanted to change. Changing lifelong patterns can be scary and seemingly impossible. He had to challenge thoughts and fears such as those by anchoring himself before, during, and after each conversation and interaction.

The process was hard and got a little worse before it got better. The emotions and mental chatter he endured felt extreme and antagonizing. Some family members were angry and confused about the changes he was making and reacted harshly to him. Situations escalated, and it became increasingly challenging for him to stay the course, but he did. He knew he had a personal responsibility to do things differently if these patterns were ever going to change. It took time and deliberate efforts to engage differently, and though the drama of the holidays wasn't much different, he knew clearly how and when to navigate these difficult situations to better take care of himself.

Most people who stay the course of this work don't come out the same on the other side. Transformation is a natural part of the process. Making room for, granting permission, and allowing the necessary time for the healing to take place will serve you best when you vow to lead a healthier life and trust the process. A commitment to this work and an assurance of your highest and best effort will grant you the stick-to-itiveness you'll need.

Growth is a catalyst for incredible change and expansion, but it may come with a price. Growth can feel confusing, uncertain, and painful. This is why it's so important to first establish the prior steps you've worked on and then assess specific areas of your life to determine how well (or not well) things are serving you. This assessment period is an opportunity for the necessary attention and awareness you need to shine light on some of your deepest thoughts, behaviors, relationships, patterns, and beliefs.

Think about it this way: in life, there are certain tasks, roles, and responsibilities that require investment from you and aren't intended to be mutual or reciprocal. If you are a parent, caregiver, or in the service industry, for instance, you are serving in one-way relationships. It comes with the territory, and expecting any else is unrealistic. However, if you consistently travel down one-way paths in most of your relationships, you'll need to look at the quality of your relationships to see why you linger in the community you do.

As you endeavor to make changes, some people in your life may be supportive and encouraging, and some may not be. The places you used to go and the things you used to do may sustain you perfectly, but they also may not. The ways you enjoy spending your time, energy, and effort may look a lot different through the course of this work. Consider the things you do, the places you frequent, and the people you surround yourself with to support you more fully as you step into your empathic gifts.

242

WHAT'S DRIVING YOU?

CONSCIOUS—*"aware of one's own existence, sensations, thoughts, surroundings, etc."*

—DICTIONARY.COM

SUBCONSCIOUS—*"the part of your mind that notices and remembers information when you are not actively trying to do so, and influences your behavior even though you do not realize it"*

—CAMBRIDGE DICTIONARY

UNCONSCIOUS—*"the part of your mind that contains feelings and thoughts that you do not know about, and that influences the way you behave"*

—CAMBRIDGE DICTIONARY

You'll recall that everything is energy. As you do this work and learn to manage differently, you will attract and be drawn to different people, experiences, places, etc. This is a natural part of the growth process, though it may feel scary, sad, confusing, or even wrong in some cases. Guilt may be an emotional undercurrent you need to process through and regulate. It's important to take your time, and be honest and forthcoming about your feelings, needs, and motives as you move forward with your decisions and changed behaviors.

There may be endings that are long overdue. You may be very ready to create some changes. Perhaps these are only temporary, only on specific occasions, or only with certain people. For example, Nate felt comfortable being around his parents during the weekdays for a few hours. The escalation came during the added pressures and exposure of the holidays. The drinking increased, the invitations were greater, and the emotions seemed heightened during these times. He also realized he felt comfortable being around his extended family on his mother's side, but not his father's. Their behaviors were different, and contact with them impacted him differently. These nuances were his to decipher and determine; no one else was capable nor responsible for clarifying or communicating them.

You may be ready for more permanent endings. You may experience a new appreciation for people, places, and things that you haven't felt in quite some time. These decisions are up to you, and it's important to assess your readiness for change and follow through as you move into a more empowered place. Take your time to assess what's going on and how you feel about all of it. Lean into healthy people and healthy coping mechanisms to boost and encourage you when you need it. Seek spiritual solace and grounding.

Some of your changes may be internal, beginning with beliefs, thoughts, and words. Consider how important it is to examine the power of your thoughts and assess what exactly it is that you're thinking about. Are your thoughts empowering ones? What are the ways you refer to yourself? Do they uplift and inspire you, or is your self-talk reflective of your perceived flaws, defects, and limitations? Do any of these change when you're around certain company? This work requires you to be gentle, compassionate, also firm and direct with yourself, as well as others. Increased self-care and deliberate practices of reflection, rest, and support with be needed.

Consider your habits and routines. Do they make you feel good and launch you into your day? Are you conducting yourself in ways that serve you? Do you want to keep doing things the same way, do them differently, or to stop doing them altogether? Where are you stuck, distracted, or out of focus? What needs your attention and consideration?

The people you hang out with or have dated, why do you keep attracting the same kind of person with a different face and name? What are you ready to do differently? What behaviors or beliefs are you buying into that keep attracting the same types of people? What's your relationship with these people, and how frequently are you with them? What are you tolerating that you shouldn't be?

Changes and endings don't have to be dramatic, messy, or mean. They can happen slowly, in levels, or almost like a dial you turn down gradually. Changed behavior happens one decision at a time—one conversation, choice, event, circumstance, or person at a time. Only you can determine who and what needs to go and who and what gets to stay. The choice is up to you.

WHERE DO I BEGIN?

Social, familial, cultural, and religious conditioning is a very real thing, and it's important to determine how this has shaped you in both healthy and unhealthy ways. From the very beginning, you experience and witness millions of small interactions, energy exchanges, engagements, and conversations, and from your young, innocent, childlike understanding, draw subtle conclusions that quickly become the lens through which you see the world and what you define as right and wrong. This becomes the foundation for your life and shapes the way you function in every arena. Some beliefs may serve you well; some probably don't. It's likely that you are holding on to several distorted or limiting perceptions that interrupt your personal power and strengths.

Such conditioning has a powerful impact in forming who you are and how you relate in the world. It's important to assess and realign your perspectives and beliefs. Most likely, you're not still reading beginner-level books. Like your capacity for reading, you've grown, expanded, matured, and changed. But has your inner script done the same? The way you see yourself, the things you're capable of, the ways you partake in life—do they support your growth, your gifts, and all that you're capable of? Is it time to rewrite and reclaim a different story line?

Beliefs and thoughts are often subtle, even subconscious. The routines, habits, relationships, and obligations you partake in may come from early socialization and training. It's likely that these are based on other people's opinions, an early experience, or a message that imprinted you somehow. Your sense of *should* may be very strong and based on others' projections, rules, and expectations. These may have become well-worn paths that don't even require your effort or conscious energy anymore. It's like muscle memory. Like an old song and dance, you simply roll through your day, exist in relationships, and make decisions without much conscious thought or effort. Until now . . .

LET IT GO

The work of an Enlightened Empath requires commitment to yourself, the process, and your gifts. It calls for honesty, insight, dedication, and personal responsibility. Surrender what you think you know, along with your attachment to these old beliefs. Loosen your grip on these perceptions. Willingness and readiness are two essential ingredients in the course of this work. Have an open mind, along with a sense of curiosity and possibility.

First, there is a critical buy-in for you to consider: you must acknowledge that *you* are the creator of your life. Incorporating a profound belief such as this will enable you to look at your life and call into consciousness the principles you want to subscribe to and those that you don't. This is your opportunity for self-reflection and self-honesty as you wipe the slate clean and step into the empowered state of self-responsibility.

With that, it's time to look at some things that have probably been around for a long time but need your attention, assessment, and redirection. Through this process, you will shine some light on the ingrained patterns, beliefs, relationships, habits, and routines that could be working against you. Perhaps you've been limiting yourself with excuses, justifications, minimizations, and distractions. Maybe you're riddled with patterns of pleasing, perfecting, or performing. We'll look at those too.

Have you ever taken the time to consider the beliefs you've bought into, your core definitions of basic life concepts, such as happiness, family, or success, the ways you've been labeled, how you've coped, or the lessons you drew from certain life experiences? That's a lot to consider and can provide a powerful starting point for understanding yourself better. Maybe those old messages of being too sensitive, crazy, mentally ill, or "too much" still haunt you. It is here that you can decide what you want to continue subscribing to and what you're ready to let go of.

This work will require some investigating, assessment, and rewriting, maybe even some endings to bring you to your full potential. Just like you outgrow many other things in life, you may find that you've outgrown certain people, places, and things that no longer serve you. This is not judgment, ridicule, or criticism, nor is it a must. It's simply coming to terms with the people and things in life that no longer fit, serve, or work well for you. It's about creating those *necessary* endings. As your energy shifts, wounds heal, and your personal narrative changes, many things are likely to change and even end.

Assessing the health of your community and connecting with like-minded people are necessary steps to fully support your empathic journey.

Imagine having an intentional community of individuals who speak your language; where you are seen, known, heard, and deeply understood; a community in which you are unconditionally accepted and fully yourself. It has been said that you are as healthy as the five people you spend the most time with. Consider that as you move forward.

Currently, I spend time with:

1.

2.

3.

4.

5.

Overall, this influences me in the following ways:

1.

2.

3.

People I like to spend time with:

1.

2.

3.

4.

5.

Conscious Community:

Your life experience is shaped by what you believe to be true and the behaviors you engage in on a regular basis. Your daily routine and the story in your mind are well rehearsed and deeply ingrained, and at this point, totally habitual. The Britannica Dictionary defines *habit* as "any regularly repeated behavior that requires little or no thought and is learned rather than innate." Cambridge Dictionary defines it as "something that you do often and regularly, sometimes without knowing that you are doing it." Consider the cumulative effects of these emotional, mental, and behavioral habits.

Of course, you're going to care about the people you connect with—you're an Empath. But caring *for* is different from care*taking*. Changing the ways you connect and relate to others can be confusing and challenging. It may take some time, and it may get a little rocky. Feelings might get hurt. Conflict may arise. Hard conversations may need to be had. Sometimes old habits die hard, and people might not respect, understand, or appreciate the changes you're making. It can feel awkward and challenging at times, but continued practice and awareness will allow you to stay the course.

Now let's pivot from the people in your life and turn the journey inward. Consciously consider your thoughts, beliefs, attitude, perspective, approach, habits, and routine. That's a lot of terrain for you to cover. What are the habits you practice? What energy do you bring to the world? When an issue presents itself, what's your first thought or visceral reaction? What are some of your motives for the things you do? How in tune are you to your own feelings and needs? How well are you taking care of yourself and allowing your well-being to be your top priority?

Next, recognizing the emotional habits you carry and the thoughts you entertain will offer a huge dose of awareness of your mental and emotional perspectives. Are you awake, alert, and alive to your inner working? What do you most want? What is life calling you toward? Are you enthusiastic and curious, or do you approach things with resistance and hesitancy, such as "Yeah, but . . ." or "I can't because . . ."?

Do you limit yourself with fear, obligation, doubt, or worry? What would life be like if you offered yourself permission, possibilities, and a sense of freedom to simply try? What would you say yes to if you flexed your courage muscle?

WHO ARE YOUR PEOPLE?

Alyanna referred to herself as a pretzel. She had spent most of her life twisting and turning herself in the most unnatural, uncomfortable ways to gain attention, approval, and acceptance. It began when she was little, trying to be everything her family thought she should be—cute, smart, helpful, reserved. She never fit their mold, but she sure twisted herself inside out trying to do so and carried that tendency into most of her adult relationships. She struggled with being the most natural thing on earth—herself—at least until she began this work.

Empaths are a unique, distinct population of folks who don't fit everywhere and with everyone. Knowing *what* to do is as important as knowing *who* to do it with. You are not a one-size-fits-all person, and you were never meant to be. You will not be everyone's cup of tea. Nor is everyone intended to be your cup of tea. The more you do this work and align with people who get and support you, the more your connections and community will change.

Allowing yourself to be with safe, respectful people who *get* you may take some time, patience, risk, vulnerability, and intentionality. You may have to stretch that familiar comfort zone. Showing up in the world fully yourself is a decision, and it may result in some emotional bumps and bruises along the way. Empaths often develop coping strategies early on—chameleon ways of fitting in—to please, perfect, and placate others, to perform based on what's expected of them or what will make others happy. Trying to show up authentically may feel incredibly risky, especially if you've felt flawed or dysfunctional.

It's critical to have a place you can call home, emotionally and physically, with a full sense of belonging with a community of people who understand, honor, and support you and your gifts and who will also challenge you and hold you accountable if needed. Building such support starts with your own acknowledgment, appreciation, and respect for who and what you are. You've worked hard to assess and clean up your belief systems. You attract what you believe, and a foundation of self-love will attract a community of people who see you as the gift you are.

If you're having a hard time finding or building such a community, it's vital to look at your beliefs about yourself, your worth, and what you bring to the table. Raise your standards. Know your worth. Have zero tolerance for self-abuse and mistreatment, and work to mend your thoughts and beliefs.

Secondly, be willing to put yourself out there. Though it can be overwhelming and scary, and you may never prefer to be the life of the party, this is an opportunity for you to practice what you've learned, with the use of your tools to find the people and experiences that align with your interests and needs. Search your community groups and be willing to try something different to find your crew. Trust Flow and those intuitive nudges when seeking direction and opportunity. Listen to your instinct, be open to Turn Right Here Adventures, and celebrate your wins by acknowledging yourself for trying something different regardless of the outcome.

My life changed the moment I started saying yes to opportunities that presented themselves, even when they scared me. If there was an intuitive nudge of curiosity, I followed through with different opportunities, events, and experiences. I was terrified, insecure, and awkward, but I went anyway and sat through the discomfort and voices of fear and doubt echoing in my mind.

It didn't come easy or naturally at first. I had to "act as if" long before my emotion and confidence caught up with me.

I can recall the first event I ever agreed to attend with this mindset. I challenged myself with this work, yet I mentally backed out of the commitment at least a dozen times. I found a hundred excuses to try to get out of going, built a pile of evidence that it was a terrible idea, and was sure I'd made the worst mistake of my life. But as I looked at the state of fear and self-doubt I was living in, I knew it would never change until I *decided* to change something. So, I went, and yes, I was scared the entire time, uncomfortable with so much "people-ing" with folks I didn't know and was horrified at the thought of doing anything outside my rigid comfort zone. But I survived. And when I explored it more honestly, I realized that I actually enjoyed it. It was a pivotal point of healing and self-discovery.

Being seen and known with a sense of belonging is what I had always longed for. Yet, decades of uncertainty and insecurity ferociously nipped at my heels, and I had to sit in the vulnerability and perceived risk of it all. I spent most of life feeling as though I was on the outside looking in, and finally, I had an opportunity to really step into the beauty of relationships. Seems silly that it was so scary, but the vulnerability still feels risky at times. I have to talk back to those feelings, or doubt and fear and keep them in check.

From that one event, I built courage and confidence while facing those ridiculous inner demons. I challenged myself and boldly took action in the face of fear and doubt. From that one experience, beautiful friendships developed that have lasted years, I was invited to more events and included in a community of amazing souls. Most importantly, an internal shift occurred, giving me the audacity to keep showing up—not only at events, but in life.

❧ TIME TO PONDER

···

Use this section to explore some of your core beliefs. This is an exercise of exploration and understanding. There is to be no judgment, and there are no right or wrong answers. You will investigate your thoughts and views to understand the tone they set. It's critical to honor the truth of your thoughts and be aware of what's fueling your mind and spirit and impacting your perspective.

Read each prompt and write down the first thing that comes to mind. Please don't evaluate or second-guess. Your answers may simply reflect your current mood or recent experience. It doesn't have to be a concrete belief; it just gives some evidence to the thoughts and ideas you have. These may reveal some insight and deeper understanding of your belief systems.

The world is _____

I am _____

People are _____

My family is _____

Men are _____

Women are _____

People tell me I am _____

I think of myself as _____

Love is _____

My biggest fear is _____

As a child, I _____

I define happiness as _____

As an Empath, I _____

I would never want someone to think of me as _____

I feel best about myself when _____

I'm drawn to people who are _____

I struggle with people who are _____

To me, energy is _____

My beliefs are healthy and productive:

☐ NOT AT ALL   ☐ SOMEWHAT   ☐ VERY MUCH

My beliefs are limiting and counterproductive:

☐ NOT AT ALL   ☐ SOMEWHAT   ☐ VERY MUCH

Unhealthy labels and beliefs I've subscribed to:

1.
2.
3.

Beliefs I'm ready to let go of:

1.
2.
3.

Beliefs I want to redefine:

1.
2.
3.

Healthy labels I've subscribed to:

1.
2.
3.

Some things in my life that need my attention:

1.
2.
3.

Some things I'm ready to do differently:

1.
2.
3.

Some things or people I'm ready to change my interactions with:

1.
2.
3.

Some things or people I'm ready to let go of:

1.
2.
3.

My strengths include:

1.
2.
3.
4.
5.

People are lucky to know me because:

1.

2.

3.

4.

5.

Because I'm living an empowered life, I no longer:

1.

2.

3.

Because I'm living an empowered life, I now:

1.

2.

3.

As you steady yourself along a new path, there may be some hard decisions, changes, and endings you need to face. You are constantly evolving, and it's your right and responsibility to claim what's in your best interest and to let go of what isn't. Because these beliefs are habitual and long-standing, repetition and rehearsal will be necessary to establish a new norm and new patterns within your brain. Take your time. If grief and adjustment are in order, know that it is perfectly fine for you to grant yourself that permission to feel whatever you need to feel and take the time to heal and acclimate.

REWIRING THE BRAIN

The following are some guidelines to assist you with changed behavior and developing new patterns:

- **Redecide**—Just because you've always done something doesn't mean you have to keep doing it. You have a right to change your mind. Know that you can "redecide" at any point. You are responsible for acting in your best interest and in the interest of the health of your relationships.
- **Self-define**—This is your ability to define major life concepts for yourself. It is the shedding of habit, early training, and exposure, along with social, cultural, and familial conditioning as you create new personal definitions of concepts like success, love, happiness, family, fun, etc.
- **Practice and repetition**—These changes won't happen over-night. Be as clear as you can about the changes you're making; take small, consistent actions of "Acting As If"; and practice these methods to establish new habits, routines, beliefs, and community.
- **Boundaries are your best friends.** Knowing how to set them and with whom is critical to your journey.
- **Identify your motives.** The health of any behavior or decision is based on your reasons for doing it. Be honest in clarifying your intentions and stand firmly in what you're doing or not doing. You can't prove your motives; you can only know them for yourself.
- **Detach and let go.** Know that everyone has a Higher Power, and quite frankly, you are not it. It is not your job to fix, heal,

or save people. Surrender the ones you love to the God of your understanding. Know that everyone has their own path to walk, and it's not up to you to decide. Commit to walking your own path and letting others walk theirs.

PERSONAL LEARNING:

CHAPTER 10

Elders & Eternal

*But a role model in the flesh provides more than
inspiration; his or her very existence is confirmation of
possibilities one may have every reason to doubt, saying,*

"Yes, someone like me can do this."

—SONIA SOTOMAYOR

No man is an island unto himself.

—JOHN DONNE

Cassandra was a very nice person. Simply put, she did what was expected of her, never made waves, and made sure others were well taken care of. She was raised in the church and taught early on that the proper order of life included #1: God, #2: Others, and #3: Self. In her sacrificial view of life and relationships, she took that message to the extreme. She feared God. From the time she was a little girl, she learned the lesson that she was an unworthy sinner who needed to get right with God. She spent every day trying to be good enough, sacrificial enough, and somehow shed the shame of unworthiness.

When tragedy struck her family, Cassandra was rocked to the core. The trauma was big, and she could not wrap her mind or her heart around it. She struggled with shock, anger, grief, and doubt about what had happened. When she revealed a glimpse of that struggle to her prayer group, they told her she needed to have more faith and trust God's will no matter what. Between their advice and Cassandra's upbringing, she had no permission to feel, no room to grieve, and no space to struggle. She had to force herself to immediately accept that what had happened was God's will; either that or she had to accept that the struggle she was experiencing was in fact owed to a lack of faith.

Cassandra was trying to digest trauma with a smile on her face and complete denial and suppression of her pain, fearing that others would see her devastation as evidence of her sinful nature. She couldn't sleep, could barely function, was distracted and consumed with painful memories, all while shaming and loathing herself for being weak. Her use of alcohol was the only way she could find to numb the pain.

Sometime after, Cassandra was charged with a DUI. Two months later, she came to see me. Her world was in shambles, and the public shame and embarrassment had her on the brink and questioning if she could go on living. She spent weeks sitting on my couch, sorting through her decline. We discussed how she'd originally found refuge in a few glasses of wine, and how those glasses quickly became bottles. Nothing seemed to numb the pain of what she had experienced, even as the voices of spiritual failure and shame haunted her. Alcohol was her only refuge, though it was a shallow one, because no substance could take away the pain she was feeling.

This rock-bottom place of devastation was a turning point for Cassandra. Not only did she commit to sort through her trauma with me but also the spiritual rigidity and fear she'd been raised with. She was terrified to express emotions, question God's plan, or demonstrate any struggle or doubt. Yet, it was this low point that allowed her to see that the path itself was killing her.

Redefining her relationship with God was harder for Cassandra than facing the pain of trauma. She feared she would be struck down, spend eternity in hell, and leave a legacy of condemnation. But she stuck with the process and came to terms with a God of her understanding—one of love, compassion, and permission to struggle. Her friends changed, her prayers changed, her worship came in a form of love like nothing she'd ever experienced before. She spent time struggling and wrestling with God, questioning, lamenting, and finally finding peace, surrender, and understanding. Cassandra's faith became profound, deep, authentic, and real. Most importantly, it was her own, not one that had been defined for or prescribed to her.

No one comes through life unscathed. Every lifetime comes with its fair share of tragedy, heartache, and challenge. Yes, you've been hurt, people have failed you, and certain things haven't worked out the way you thought they should have. Experiences such as these can be devastating and shape and define how you understand, define, and relate to God. The way people respond to your emotions, reactions, and needs can be equally impactful.

You are a spiritual being having a human experience, a soul with a mind and a body. You are here to learn, grow, and expand. You are alive for a reason, and nothing that's occurred has been wrong or a mistake. The Source who created the world also created you. There is divine purpose.

Your spiritual path is a personal one. There is mystery, pain, loss, awe, and so much that is unknown about God, heaven, angels, prayer, death, or if there's a hell, much less any type of spiritual purpose you are meant to serve while you're here. There's meaning to it, and that meaning is for *you* to determine. There are lessons and opportunities that are uniquely yours to do with what you will. Some lessons you've faced repeatedly.

You were beautifully made for a soul purpose and divine journey. You can do it alone, but you don't have to; you can tune in to Higher provision, invite the God of your understanding in, and ask for support and guidance at any point. Spirit works more easily where it is invited and welcomed.

In this section, you will explore your understanding of God (however you may define that understanding) and decide what type of relationship you want to have, if any at all. Most people hold fast to spiritual beliefs they were taught. Have you ever assessed how true those beliefs are for you? Have you considered your relationship with the God of your understanding? You can do that here with a fine-tooth comb to see what you want to let go and what you want to explore further.

LEAN ON ME

If you do not trust life to unfold, the mind takes over and it becomes a game of strategy, motivated by anxiety. The mistrust is unfair. Life has given us so us much, and yet we do not trust it.

—MOOJI

TRUST—*"to believe someone is good and honest and will not harm you, or that something is safe and reliable"*

—CAMBRIDGE DICTIONARY

How many times have you heard the stories of someone enduring life's tragic endeavors only to hear years later the number of gifts, lessons, or blessings that stemmed from those seemingly unbearable circumstances? How many times has a friend or family member endured a breakup, financial hardship, or job loss they feel devastated and humiliated by, but from the outside, you can already see what a good thing this is for them and know they would never have made those changes on their own? How many times have you faced a situation you thought you might never overcome, and as the years unfolded, you were able to see clearly how it shaped and defined you and brought you to things you might not have ever otherwise experienced?

I will never make light of someone's pain, perspective, or loss. Crisis and trauma are real dynamics that can alter the course of one's life, and they need the time, space, and permission to grieve and process as much as they need to. Trying to move someone too quickly to the bright side of things can be dismissive and further damaging. Healing takes its own time and course, and during the process, it's critical to assess the beliefs, coping mechanisms, support systems, and perspective you have, as it will highly influence the meaning and purpose you draw from adversity.

You may have a hard time trusting life. Maybe you were exposed at a young age to looming uncertainty that instilled a need to control or a fear that if things won't go the way you want them to, you might miss out on something important, or you won't be safely taken care of. From that place, patterns and beliefs began to take shape on a very subconscious level, laying the foundation for how you function in the world. Once fear is introduced and settles in as the norm, your sense of safety, stability, and security have not proven to be reliable or readily available. Survival is linked to control, self-will, and self-determination, allowing the ego to run rampant.

It is possible to heal from that pain, fear, and uncertainty. If you never had a soft, safe place to land or a haven to lean into when life got scary and hard, it may seem risky and vulnerable to incorporate a different perspective as you learn to trust life. Rather than continuing these patterns, let's imagine a very different belief system you can begin to practice and lean into. This is a set of beliefs creating a solid foundation that allows you a safe, trusting place of assurance and possibilities, even when it seems like things are falling apart.

I understand why people have a hard time trusting. Life may feel like it's disappointed and failed you. Trusting yourself, others, a Higher Being, or life can feel vulnerable, naïve, and counterintuitive. Humility and openness may be associated with weakness. Control and self-will can provide the illusion of armor and strength but also run along the shore of Force.

Remember the trust fall we talked about? If you've experienced loss, trauma, betrayal, and turmoil, trying to lean into trust and assurance may terrify you or evoke panic and doubt. You may scoff at the idea and recite dozens of reasons why life cannot be trusted and is not working in your best interest. It can be hard to trust and feel guided when life delivers messages through hardship, feeling like a baseball bat upside the head or a nicely delivered shit sandwich you somehow need to swallow and digest. You may question, "How can this possibly be a good thing that life is trying to offer and teach?"

Tragedy, hardship, and crisis are often taken very personally. The brain wants to understand things that happen and assign reason and meaning. The brain constantly draws conclusions, often faulty ones, about why something is happening. It's a common conclusion that somehow, you've done something wrong or have somehow caused the hardship. Though it's important to assess your part and any possible reasons, crisis is not always about cause and effect. It can, however, serve a purpose if you process it with that deep-seated trust.

People interpret their struggles as failure, incompetence, unworthiness, undeserving, punishment, not doing enough, or somehow having done something wrong. It can seem impossible to draw positives out of tragic circumstances, and people sometimes try to do this too soon, far before someone has properly grieved or processed enough to see any light at the end of the tunnel. Strife, loss, and hardship can trigger a lot of old wounds, stories, fears, and beliefs that are essential to assess, heal, and clarify.

Developing a trusting relationship with life will change your perspective and allow you deeper trust and understanding in the face of crisis. Learning to work in conjunction with life, accepting its guidance and direction, may take time, patience, and practice. Your behavior will be different, cleaner, and healthier as you no longer want to wrangle life to try to get things to go the way you want them to go. Like that dreaded trust fall and the horrible fear of falling straight on your tail, you may resort to old patterns of Force as you try to fix, manage, and control what's happening around you. Just like developing a relationship with Flow and intuition, this deep-seated trust in life is about consistent practice.

ETERNAL

Our eternal spiritual self is more real than anything we perceive in this physical realm and has a divine connection to the infinite love of the Creator.

—EBEN ALEXANDER

ETERNAL—*"without beginning or end; lasting forever; always existing"*

—DICTIONARY.COM

What do you believe about the spirit world? Do you have trust in a Higher Power, even when things don't seem to make any sense? Do you feel loved and assured, or do you struggle with a sense of unworthiness and condemnation? Do you seek spiritual input or direction?

What's your process for doing that? Are you listening to what God / Life / Spirit is trying to tell you, or do you resist or feel uncertain and confused? Are there nudges, hints, and suggestions being offered to you? Are you paying attention to those, or are you determined in your own will, timing, and course?

Whatever you believe is completely up to you, but it's important to recognize the beliefs you're subscribing to and how well they're serving you. You don't have to hold any beliefs or maintain any relationship with a Higher Power, but it makes life a whole lot easier if you do. No one can assign a God or religion to you, and what you learned when you were younger may not be what you want to continue to participate in.

Regardless of your circumstances, developing a deep assurance in a power greater than yourself will allow you to work in alignment with a profound, steadfast spiritual realm rather than fighting your way, alone, upstream. Of course, this does not mean that everything will always go your way, or that you will never face hardship. Deliberately stated again, life works in your favor whether you know it or not, even when it comes delivered in that proverbial shit sandwich that life sometimes serves up.

Life often works like this: the nudge begins with a gentle whisper or nod that you overlook, minimize, deny, or excuse. Then the volume or the heat turns up a bit and nudges you more firmly, and still you persist in your ways. Life continues to direct, redirect, and communicate, but you trudge along, insisting you know what's best. Life is often left no choice but to provide the clobber effect with a baseball bat right upside the noggin to deliver the same point it was trying to deliver in much gentler way before.

You have free will and permission to live your life as you see fit. Spirit goes where it is invited and allowed in. Your spirit guides and ancestors are the same way. Asking for insight, direction, wisdom, and clarity can open you up to a much deeper level of support and assistance as you learn to lean into spiritual guidance. Have prayerful conversations with your Higher Power to seek wisdom, and if you're willing, develop a practice of tuning in and asking for help.

Learn to ask soulful questions in your writing and meditation such as:

- Where do you want me?
- How can I best serve?
- What is the option that serves most?
- What do I need to do?

Offer prayerful statements such as:

- Guide me to what's best for me.
- Close doors I am not meant to walk through.
- I am willing and trusting.

SOMEWHERE ALONG THE WAY

Travis and his family went to church every Sunday, and he attended a Catholic school. Father David was a teacher, coach, and favorite confidant to most of the kids in the school. He was very different from the other teachers and would often poke fun of religion, the principal, other staff, and the rules that no one seemed to understand. Father David was a trusted leader, great listener, authority figure, and upstanding member of the church. Travis and his parents thought nothing of it when Father David offered to drive Travis home after practice.

Twenty-eight years later, as he sat in my office, Travis unloaded layers of pain, anguish, and confusion about a trusted leader and confidant who had taken advantage of him under the guise of God and religion. Travis had never told anyone. Instead, he cursed and swore off anything having to do with the church or God. He struggled to understand how a man of God could do something like that to an innocent, naïve child. The shame and rage he carried all those years consumed him and blocked any understanding of spirituality, intimacy, vulnerability, and trust. He was confused, hurt, and ashamed. It took a great deal of processing and even deeper healing to separate human behavior from a Source greater than him. Some people never get to that point where Travis was finally able to.

The world can be an incredibly hard place. People cause great pain in and out of the church. Sometimes, the people who claim to be the holiest are the ones who hurt and judge the most. Sometimes, things happen that leave you wondering, *What kind of God would allow this to happen?* Perhaps you've had life experiences that wounded you deeply and soured your perspective of God, church, or religion. It's possible that these wounds caused by church people or other religious experiences have tainted your spiritual understanding. But it's important to remember that people are people; they are not God. They should not be mistaken with anything holy, mighty, or powerful. If you carry wounds from people, experiences, or church, those wounds need to be separated from the way you feel about your actual Higher Power. They may be very interwoven, but it is time to tease them apart, to heal what needs your attention, and to define your beliefs.

Further, how you've experienced your parents is likely to be projected onto your view of God. If you had an absent, controlling father, you're likely to see God with some of the same qualities. If you experienced your household to be safe, consistent, and reliable, you'll have an easier time with the idea of a dependable God. If you have unresolved issues or other spiritual gunk, you probably have some stuff that needs to be sorted through. This process is enlightening and necessary.

What's your response when you hear words like *obey, submit, surrender, conform*? Concepts such as these may be hard for you to comprehend and relate to. They may be knowingly or unknowingly woven into your understanding of God and/or religion. These concepts have sometimes been used too rigidly, creating fear, misuse, and misrepresentation of a Higher Power, rules, rituals, and personal worth. Your perception, beliefs, and experiences may be filled with hurt, confusion, and resistance to anything considered holy. You may take these concepts a little too far for your own good and have a rigid or absolute understanding.

When you've filtered through all your spiritual residue, you're more likely to comply and submit to the guidance and direction of a Higher Power you trust because you feel loved, seen, and accepted. Working in unison with a Higher Source allows you to practice Flow much more easily and quickly. Leaning into intuitive nudges and synchronicities is much easier when you believe your God has your best interest in mind and is looking out for you rather than scrutinizing or punishing you at every turn. Spiritual alignment offers opportunities for guidance and input, directing you, like breadcrumbs along a trail leading you in specific directions.

Surrender may be one of the hardest concepts to consider. Maybe you confuse this with failure, loss, or defeat. Yet, it simply means to stop resisting. As you further your spiritual walk and sort through your concept of God, you'll gladly surrender as a method of release and acceptance. You'll see patterns of Force almost as soon as you start doing them, and you become willing to let go much more easily. That may take some practice and rewriting of the internal script.

271

YOU GET WHAT YOU LOOK FOR

Where you look is where you go. You'll see evidence of what you believe to be true. If you think the world is a horrible place, you'll see proof everywhere you turn. If you believe that people are awful, you only have to turn on the news to be flooded with stories of such. If you look for things that are good, that you can be happy about, or ways that people are kind, you'll see just as much confirmation of those views. Your belief systems shape the way you see the world, the decisions you make, and your ability to connect and relate.

How entrenched are you in your belief systems about God? Have you stopped to assess how well they're serving you? Are the ideas you hold your own, or are they based on traumatic experiences or things you were taught by others? What's your understanding of worship, faith, obedience, and relationship?

Organized religion has constructed stories, tradition, rules, expectations, and lessons for generations. Some of these are loving, encouraging, supportive messages about basic conduct and mindset, along with how to be in relationship with one another. Other messages are condemning, rigid, and fear based. Take the time to assess your perspective and belief systems to clarify what you align with. You may need to tease apart your worldly experiences with people and man-made rules from the spiritual relationship you want to be able to have.

You may connect and resonate with organized religion, and you may not. Your spiritual practice and relationship are for you to define and determine. If you're confused or bogged down by old messages and expectations, or you have endured trauma or painful experiences in the name of anything holy, those deserve your full attention, respect, and reflection.

WHAT DO YOU THINK?

You get to decide what's right for you. Self-defining is the process of clarifying life concepts in ways that are accurate and true for you. This is your opportunity to self-define the God of your understanding. Maybe you've adopted beliefs and practices from outside sources. Past experiences, childhood learning, and family role modeling weigh heavily on what you think and what you believe. There comes a point in life where you have full permission to decide for yourself, and that time is now.

A tree with no deep roots will not sustain the storm. How deeply are you rooted in your faith and relationship with a Higher Power? Take the time you need to clarify and sort through your concept of God. I encourage you to wrestle things out with God, express your confusion or pain, and ask the necessary questions to heal or resolve your struggles. Having a spiritual relationship that is built on your principles and desires allows you to feel certain and assured in deepening your spiritual journey, rather than living with faith that requires your submission and obedience without a personal relationship. The time you take to sort through your "God stuff" will allow you to build trust, connection, understanding, and intimacy with a Source much greater than you.

Spirituality is one of the most intimate relationships you can have. No one else can define your beliefs and preferences. You can borrow the faith of someone else if you don't have any clear concepts or aren't quite ready to commit to any particular idea. It can be Christ, a tree, Source, meditation practice, Buddha—it really doesn't matter. This is a Higher Power that you develop a loving, trusting relationship with and feel connected to. A consistent practice of stillness, prayer, meditation, or worship will allow you the quality time to develop deeper roots and a healthier connection.

❧ SPIRITUALITY

....

To me, spirituality is:

_____

_____

_____

I was taught the following about God:

_____

_____

_____

The God of my understanding is:

_____

_____

_____

The God of my understanding isn't:

_____

_____

_____

I am connected to the God of my understanding:

☐ NOT AT ALL   ☐ SOMEWHAT   ☐ VERY MUCH

I have issues and struggles with God:

☐ NOT AT ALL   ☐ SOMEWHAT   ☐ VERY MUCH

My issues with God include:

1. _____

2. _____

3. _____

My issues with spirituality include:

1.
2.
3.

My spiritual practices include:

1.
2.
3.

I feel spiritually connected when:

1.
2.
3.

I want to experience God as:

PERSONAL LEARNING:

ELDERS—THOSE WHO HAVE GONE BEFORE

Headline news: you never have to do this work alone, and you are as healthy as the community you surround yourself with. As you grow in your understanding of and appreciation for your wiring and strengths, you will be able to build connection with people who support and inspire you. Perhaps you're being called to try new things, go different places, step outside of your comfort zone, or reestablish your tribe. Building quality relationships may take time and intentional effort. The key focus is quality, not quantity. You may find that your circle becomes small but deepens in connection and conversation.

Assessing your community is as important as assessing your thoughts, energy, and environment. Be aware and selective as you build new connections. Take your time. Be willing to take chances, put yourself out there, and risk not liking something so you can be clearer about what you do like. Being told no or having something seemingly not work out is just information that points you in a different direction. Childhood bravery and innocence are a great way to approach new people and new opportunities. Have an open mind and be willing to see where curiosity and connection may lead you. There's no failure, no wrong directions, and no mistakes—just exploration and learning.

Your commitment to growth and development will propel you into new opportunities that will challenge and even scare you a bit. Don't settle or try to fit somewhere you don't. A steadfast assurance that you are capable and worthy of great things will empower you along the way.

You might consider choosing a mentor or role model, as they can offer a stabilizing force as you adapt to the changes and necessary steps of this work. Lean into people who've walked the walk to offer inspiration and assurance that you can do it too. If you know someone locally who might make for a strong mentor or role model, meet with them, buy them a cup of coffee, invite them for a walk. Open yourself up to quality experiences and stay present with the thoughts and feelings that surface. You'll know clearly if this is someone you can connect with or not. Don't be afraid to ask, invest in sessions or a class, try something new, and feel the vulnerability of it. It may be the most transformative risk you take.

There are many folks who've come before you and paved their way through this work. There is no need to travel alone or try to reinvent the wheel. Having someone to look to for a steadfast example will stabilize and assure you, giving you support and encouragement while offering a road map for your possibilities and path.

Beyond anything else, know that you are not alone. You have resources, support, and guidance available in multiple capacities to access at any point. They are awaiting your invitation daily. It only requires your openness and willingness. Whether it's God, guides and leaders who've traveled the road before you, ancestors, spirit guides, angels, or whatever you are willing to tap into, they're available to you at any point. Learning to access, lean into, and develop an intimate relationship with these sources and guides allows you to embrace a deeper layer of growth and trust.

Having walked this path, I am committed to walk with others and am happy to serve in any capacity to spread the word, grow this work, and empower you and fellow Empaths so we can stand together. You and I can design your path through individual sessions, coaching courses, and group experiences. The Empowered Empath is a course I teach, where this work all began with other folks who needed community, insight, growth, and support much like you might. I am here to help and serve however I can.

The following is a list of gurus who've effectively put their creative stamp on the world. They have different styles, techniques, and personalities. It's not one-size-fits-all, so explore each one and trust yourself to access the right resource at the right time. Remember, it's all practice, exploration, and learning. You are your wisest guide, able to discern and decide for yourself.

WISE TEACHERS

Louise Hay	Judith Orloff	Judy Dyer
Sydney Campos	Deepak Chopra	Pam Grout
Abraham Hicks	Maryann Williamson	Maya Angelou
Wayne Dyer	Dr. Joe Dispenza	Dr. Sue Morter
Kyle Cease	Dr. Daniel Amen	Brené Brown
Lee Harris	Christ	Buddha
Angels	Gaia TV	Ancestors

❧ SPIRITUAL LEADERS

....

Connection with others is important to me:

☐ NOT AT ALL   ☐ SOMEWHAT   ☐ VERY MUCH

The quality of my relationships with others is:

☐ STRUGGLING   ☐ SO-SO   ☐ STRONG

I'm drawn to people who are:

1.

2.

3.

People I admire:

1.

2.

3.

My role models and greatest teachers:

1.

2.

3.

Lessons I learned from them:

1.

2.

3.

Qualities I offer others:

1.

2.

3.

Qualities I want to develop within myself:

1.

2.

3.

PERSONAL LEARNING:

CONCLUSION

*I am only one, but still I am one. I cannot do everything,
but still I can do something.*

—EDWARD EVERETT HALE

*. . . because the ones who are crazy enough to think that
they can change the world are the ones who do.*

—STEVE JOBS

*One tree can start a forest;
One smile can begin a friendship;
One hand can lift a soul;
One word can frame the goal;
One act can inspire a movement
One candle can wipe out darkness;
One laugh can conquer gloom;
One hope can raise your spirits;
One touch can show you care;
One life can make the difference.
Be that one today!*

—AUTHOR UNKNOWN

As we draw this work to a close, I want to acknowledge the path you're on and celebrate all that you've done and the courage it takes to show up. I want to thank you for rising to a higher calling. Rest assured, the world needs you, your gifts, and the purpose you're here to serve.

It is my honor and privilege to walk with you during this time. Now, more than ever, the world needs you at your highest and best. A committed practice to each of these areas will continue to strengthen and empower you. My hope is that you continue to grow, expand, play, and explore. Also, I hope that you share with the world so you can now Educate, Equip, and Empower others.

Let's work together. Share your successes and struggles.

Find out more at AllysonBlythe.com.

❧ PERSONAL COMMITMENTS

....

I am:

_____

_____

_____

_____

_____

I am grateful for:

_____

_____

_____

_____

_____

To me, Enlightenment means:

_____

_____

_____

_____

_____

_____

As an Enlightened Empath, I:

_____

_____

_____

_____

_____

My commitment to myself:

My commitment to this practice:

MY PERSONAL LEARNING:

ALLYSON BLYTHE has always known that she was made to do this work. After earning her master's degree at Syracuse University, she opened her private practice in 2000. With a heart for the underdog, an unwavering drive for helping others, and a soul that draws on deep wisdom, insight, and intuition, Allyson has dedicated her career to the mission of Educating, Equipping, and Empowering others to dig deep into self-awareness, emotional intelligence, self-care, and personal responsibility.

In addition to her private practice, Allyson offers seminars, workshops, group coaching, and education from the stage as a public speaker. *The ALLY Effect* is her podcast, where she Educates, Equips, and Empowers listeners to Authentically Live Life Your Way. She is also the author of *Misunderstood: Rewriting the Rules of Dignity and Self-Respect*, which serves as a powerful road map for managing life and relationships. When she is not busy impacting lives in the office, you can find her somewhere on her yoga mat or out in nature.

www.ingramcontent.com/pod-product-compliance
Lightning Source LLC
Chambersburg PA
CBHW021613120626
46545CB00001B/202